A PROBLEMATIC PATRIARCH

JONATHAN HARRIS

*(with brief outlines of the lives
of his seventeen children)*

A PROBLEMATIC PATRIARCH

JONATHAN HARRIS

*(with brief outlines of the lives
of his seventeen children)*

GARRY MOORE

Copyright © Garry Moore 2022
Cover design, Typesetting: Working Type Studio
(www.workingtype.com.au)

The right of Garry Moore to be identified as the Author of the Work has been asserted in accordance with the Copyright, Designs and Patents Act 1988.

All rights reserved. No part of this publication may be reproduced, stored in a retrieval system, or transmitted in any form or by any means without the prior written permission of the publisher, nor be otherwise circulated in any form of binding or cover other than that in which it is published and without a similar condition being imposed on the subsequent purchaser.

Garry Moore
A Problematic Patriarch: Jonathan Harris
(with brief outlines of the lives of his seventeen children)
ISBN: 978-0-6455762-0-7

CONTENTS

Introduction	1
Jonathan Harris	3
Jonathan Harris' Children	47
Jonathan Harris Jnr	49
Elizabeth Clark (née Harris)	53
Henry Harris	55
Sophia Fraser (née Harris)	59
Thomas Harris	61
George Jarvis Harris	65
William Thomas Harris	69
George Robert Grubb Harris	71
Edward Harris	73
Walter Harris	75
Francis Harris	79
Albert Harris	81
Frances Alice McEwan (née Harris)	83
Frederick Harris	85
John Phillip Harris	87
Charlotte Rebecca O'Brien (née Harris)	89
Lucy Rosetta McLeod (née Harris)	91
Appendix	95
Genealogical Charts	99
Maps, Plans, Drawings and Photos	103

Introduction

Jonathan Harris was first and foremost a convict; transported from his native Sussex in England to far off New South Wales for life in 1826 following his conviction for burglary the previous year.

In his *Botany Bay: The Real Story*, Alan Frost wrote:

> "It is one of the abiding myths of Australian history that many of those sentenced to transportation were poor people convicted of stealing a loaf of bread to feed their starving family, or a handkerchief worth a few pennies; that they were the hapless victims of a savage penal code and an uncaring, class-driven society. It seems not to matter how often or with what clarity the real situation is explained. This myth is, it seems, necessary to the maintenance of our identity as a nation forged out of dastardly oppression.
>
> It would be silly to claim that there were never miscarriages of justice, or that harsh penalties were not given for what we would now consider minor offences. Long sentences given to children or to those made desperate by poverty still trouble the mind and hurt the heart. However, the plain fact is that the majority of eighteenth-century convicts sentenced to transportation were convicted of crimes that we continue to consider serious."[1]

The offence which saw Jonathan transported for life to New South Wales was indeed a serious one. However, it is not difficult to uncover the desperate poverty which blighted his early life.

Jonathan's background in Sussex was likely one of abject poverty. Not only was he himself a lawbreaker, but so too was his mother and at least one of his half brothers. In her work *Vandemonians: The Repressed History Of Colonial Victoria*, Janet McCalman noted that:

> "What was distinctive about convicts, what separated them from their peers who had avoided the punitive power of the state, was that in the background of their offending lay a family crisis of death or desertion, a failure of the household to support its members both materially and psychologically. Loss of one parent thrust the survivor into peril; of having to care for children while working as a father; of losing all entitlement to support as a mother in a world where women were meant to be supported by men — husbands, fathers, brothers, employers…. The vulnerability was increased by the instability and insecurity of neighbourhoods. Destitution, alcohol and violence fed off each other and compounded the damage they inflicted on the young and the unprotected. These were the intimate push factors for

---

1   See Alan Frost, *Botany Bay: The Real Story* (2012), p. 54.

offending amidst the larger pressure of a rapidly changing economy. The convict's plea in mitigation was one of misfortune, abandonment, abuse, neglect and destitution: human flotsam and jetsam caught in the massive transformation of the industrial and agricultural revolutions, the pursuit of empire and the insatiable hunger for land."[2]

As will be seen below, the young Jonathan's early circumstances were ones which in substance mirrored McCalman's analysis here.

Many of those transported from Britain and Ireland to New South Wales served their sentences, attained their freedom and thereafter led blameless lives. Not so Jonathan Harris. In 1842, he was convicted after a Parramatta Quarter Sessions trial of robbery and sentenced to be again transported; on this occasion, to Van Diemen's Land for 15 years.

Jonathan secured a Conditional Pardon whilst living and working in Hobart in April 1851. During 1856 or early 1857, he secured a passage for himself, his third wife and their two young children across Bass Strait from Tasmania to Victoria. Thereafter, he moved quickly to settle in Benalla, where he spent the balance of his working life as a market gardener. He died in Benalla in 1891 at the ripe old age of 91 years.

Jonathan Harris' life as a convict and transportee was remarkable in its own right. Equally remarkable is the fact that he contracted three marriages over the course of his lifetime and sired a total of 17 children. In the main, the life led by each of these children was quite different from that led by his or her siblings and by Jonathan. Many went on to have large families in their own right, and there are no doubt very many Australians alive today who can trace their ancestry back to Jonathan Harris. Time has rendered him the patriarch of a very large Australian family.

My object in this work is not only to trace Jonathan's life, but also to provide brief sketches of the lives of all 17 of his sons and daughters.

Janet McCalman has observed:

> "Historians continue to wrestle with the character of the convicts, the significance of their contribution to the history of settler colonialism, the extent of their role in our economic development, and, indeed, such elusive phenomena as the Australian legend, our language, our self image and our soul."[3]

---

2   See Janet McCalman, *Vandemonians: The Repressed History Of Colonial Victoria* (2021), p. 38. McCalman further noted that:
    "some convicts did learn their trade from their parents.... Some were in family businesses of animal theft for butchers, or smuggling.... Brothers often worked crimes together, and young people, as everywhere, sought courage in gangs both small and large."
    See McCalman, *op. cit.*, pp. 20-21.
3   See McCalman, *op. cit.*, p. 237.

Jonathan Harris
(1800 – 1891)

Jonathan Harris was born in the English County of Sussex a little before 12 October 1800. Almost certainly born illegitimate, he was the only child of Philadelphia Allchorne and John Harris.[4]

Jonathan's mother, Philadelphia Allchorne, was born Philadelphia Newnham in 1769 in or near to the small village of Isfield in Sussex. She was baptised in the Church of St Margaret of Antioch, Isfield on 26 March 1769.[5] Although some doubt presently remains with respect to Philadelphia's antecedents, her immediate ancestors were probably born and lived their lives within a radius of 20 km of Uckfield in Sussex.

The lives of Jonathan's father, John Harris, and the latter's ancestors, have proven difficult to trace.[6] However, it would appear that John was baptised in St Mary the Virgin's Church, Ringmer, Sussex on 21 January 1773.[7] His immediate ancestors were likely born and lived their lives in Ringmer and in other parts of East Sussex.

Philadelphia Newnham clearly received no formal education. From an early age, she was probably required to assist her mother with home duties and the care of her younger siblings. This ended when she married her first husband, Thomas Allchorne on 11 October 1787 in St Margaret of Antioch's Church, Isfield.[8] Philadelphia was 18 years of age when she married. Her new husband was 29 years old.

Thomas Allchorne was born in or close to the village of Buxted in Sussex. He was christened in St Margaret the Queen's Church, Buxted on 15 August 1756.[9] It is likely that Thomas, like most of his male forebears, worked as a labourer around Buxted. It is equally likely the Philadelphia spent virtually all of her married life with Thomas in the vicinity of that village.

Philadelphia had three known children by Thomas. All were christened in St Margaret the Queen's Church,

---

4   See *Family Search: England, Sussex, Parish Registers, 1538-1910 – Jonathan Harris* (http://tinyurl.com/y9nz9dae) (at 13 August 2020).

5   Isfield is a small village on the River Ouse some 4.5 km to the south-west of the town of Uckfield. Reputedly, King Harold spent the night in the village before the Battle of Hastings in 1066: see *Wikipedia – Isfield* (http://tinyurl.com/ybm2r6bh) (at 13 August 2020); and *The Weald: Town History, Bibliography and Topography – Isfield* (http://tinyurl.com/y9s9sehn) (at 13 August 2020). See also the East Sussex Map below.

6   The problems associated with tracing Jonathan Harris' ancestry are ably canvassed in *WikiTree – John Harris (abt. 1773-abt. 1845)* (http://tinyurl.com/ycrwsmx7) (at 13 August 2020).

7   See *Family Search: Parish Registers and Poor Law Records for Ringmar – John Harris* (http://tinyurl.com/y8ne4ep8) (at 13 August 2020); and *Sussex Family History Group ("SFHG"): Ringmer St Mary the Virgin 1752-1812 – John Harris* (http://tinyurl.com/ydbnzpzk) (at 13 August 2020). Ringmer lies some 9 km to the south-south-west of Uckfield.

8   See *The Weald: People, History and Genealogy – Thomas Allchorne* (http://tinyurl.com/yc6hfq5f) (at 13 August 2020).

9   See *Family Search: Parish Registers for Buxted, 1568-1881 – Thomas Allchorne* (http://tinyurl.com/ybsl8n7u) (at 14 August 2020). Over time, Thomas' baptismal surname, and those of his descendants in the male line, has come to be spelled in a number of different ways, including : Alchorne", "Allcorn", "Alcorn" and "Allchin".

Buxted is a small village lying around 3 km to the north-east of Uckfield. Dating back to Saxon times, it was an early centre of the English iron-making industry. The first cast iron cannon made in England was said to have been cast in Buxted in 1543: see *Wikipedia – Buxted* (http://tinyurl.com/y7s29cfn) (at 14 August 2020); and *The Weald: Town History, Bibliography and Topography – Buxted* (http://tinyurl.com/yd4cjfxy) (at 12 August 2020).

Buxted.[10] The first, Thomas Allchorne Jnr, was so christened on 13 April 1788.[11] On 21 November 1820, the younger Thomas married a Jane Killick in St Margaret the Queen's Church, Buxted.[12] The *1841 England Census* had the pair living on *Connott's Farm* near Buxted, with Thomas being described as the "Farmer".[13] Thomas Allchorne Jnr died at the age of 78 years and was buried in the churchyard of Buxted's St Mary's Church on 30 June 1866.[14]

Philadelphia and Thomas' middle child, George Allchorne, was born a little before 5 January 1794 and was christened on the date.[15] He grew up to become a ploughman, no doubt employed on farms in the neighbourhood of Buxted. On 26 May 1822, George married Frances Relph in St Thomas-à-Beckett's Church, Brightling, Sussex.[16] His subsequent life is further dealt with in some detail below.

John Allchorne was the youngest child born to Philadelphia and Thomas. He was baptised on 16 April 1797.[17] John probably worked as a farm labourer in the Buxted district. He lived a comparatively short life, dying at the age of 34 in April 1831. John was buried in the churchyard of St Mary's Church, Buxted on 21 April 1831.[18]

Thomas Allchorne Snr died when his youngest son was less than six months old. He was buried at St Mary's Church in Buxted on 1 October 1797. He was but 41 years of age when he died.[19]

Thomas' death left Philadelphia with three young children, one a babe in arms. Having lost her bread-winner, her economic circumstances would have been precarious to say the least. Although she may have remained in the home where she had been living in Buxted with her late husband, it seems more likely that necessity would have caused her to move with her children from Buxted back to Isfield to live with her widowed mother or other local relatives.

Within a few short years of Thomas Allchorne's death, Philadelphia formed a relationship with John Harris. In 1800, she appears to have commenced preparations to marry the latter in St Mary the Virgin's Church in John's home village of Ringmer. The Parish Register for that Church contains an uncompleted and undated marriage banns entry from 1800 for Philadelphia and John. However, there is no mention of the publication of any marriage banns or of a bishop's licence for the two to marry.[20] It seems almost certain that no marriage between Philadelphia and John ever eventuated. Nevertheless, the relationship did produce a son, Jonathan Harris.

It is not clear where Jonathan Harris was born. If his mother remained in Buxted after Thomas Allchorne's death, she may have given birth to Jonathan there. Alternatively, she may have been living with John in Ringmer at the time of Jonathan's birth. However, it appears most likely that Jonathan would have been born in his mother's home village of Isfield, where Philadelphia would have had the assistance of her immediate relatives with the birth and in caring for her older children. What is clear is that Jonathan was baptised in St Dunstan's Church, Mayfield on 12 October 1800.[21]

---

10   See *The Weald: People, History and Genealogy – Thomas Allchorne* (http://tinyurl.com/yc6hfq5f) (at 14 August 2020); and *WikiTree – Philadelphia (Newnham) Vinall (1769-1853)* (http://tinyurl.com/ycgz3w78) (at 14 August 2020).

11   See *Family Search: England Births and Christenings, 1538-1975 – Thomas Alchorne* (http://tinyurl.com/yclqxfh5) (at 14 August 2020).

12   See *Family Search: England Marriages, 1538-1973 – Thomas Allchorne* (http://tinyurl.com/y7c77dnr) (at 14 August 2020).

13   See *Ancestry: 1841 England Census for Thomas Alchorne* (http://tinyurl.com/ycq66r6d) (at 14 August 2020).

14   See *Family Search: England, Sussex, Parish Registers, 1538-1910 – Thomas Alchorne* (http://tinyurl.com/y7mhdnmo) (at 14 August 2020).

15   See *Family Search: England Births and Christenings, 1538-1975 – George Allchorne* (http://tinyurl.com/ydx4xrkw) (at 14 August 2020).

16   See *Family Search – Frances Relph (1799-1884)* (http://tinyurl.com/y8346hl5) (at 14 August 2020). Brightling is a village lying about 20 km to the east of Uckfield and some 11.5 km to the south-east of Mayfield.

17   See *The Weald: People, History and Genealogy – John Alcorne* (http://tinyurl.com/yxoae43p) (at 14 August 2020).

18   *Ibid.*

19   See *SFHG: Buxted St Mary 1745-1899 – Thomas Allcorn* (http://tinyurl.com/y9u4dxdr) (at 14 August 2020);

20   See *Family Search: Parish Registers and Poor Law Records for Ringmer – John Harris and Philadelphia Allcorn* (http://tinyurl.com/ycmpc66d) (at 14 August 2020); and *WikiTree – Philadelphia (Newnham) Vinall (1769-1853)* (http://tinyurl.com/ycgz3w78) (at 14 August 2020).

21   See *Family Search: England, Sussex, Parish Registers, 1538-1910 – Jonathan Harris* (http://tinyurl.com/y9nz9dae) (at 14 August 2020). See also photo 1 below. The village of Mayfield lies some 13 km to the north-east of Uckfield: see *Wikipedia – Mayfield and Five Ashes* (http://tinyurl.com/y9l2fgs5) (at 14 August 2020); and *The Weald: Town History, Bibliography and Topography – Mayfield* (http://tinyurl.com/y9ouewmt) (at 14 August 2020).

In the St Dunstan's Baptism Records entry for Jonathan Harris, his parents were said to be "John and Philadelphia Harris".[22] As one website also points out, Jonathan was not listed as being illegitimate, presumably because his parents indicated to the Church's authorities that they were married even though they almost certainly weren't.[23] The same website goes on to perceptively observe that:

> "The reason for the baptism occurring in Mayfield is unknown. It may have been because John and Philadelphia were avoiding Isfield (Philadelphia's home village) and Ringmer because of the uncertain marriage status, or Mayfield was close to Buxted where Philadelphia had previously been living…."[24]

Philadelphia's relationship with John Harris proved to be a short one. In 1801, John apparently fathered a child with a Mary Tutt of Chiddingly, Sussex.[25] On 11 October 1801, also given the name "Mary", was christened in St Mary the Virgin's Church, Ringmer. The St Mary's Baptism Records originally named the parents as "John and Mary Tutt". However, the record was subsequently amended, with the name "Harris" added in different ink after the name "Tutt".[26] The younger Mary would naturally have been Jonathan Harris' half-sister. Interestingly, Jonathan's Tasmanian criminal records note that he had a sister named "Mary" at his "native place".[27]

It has been suggested that the circumstances surrounding the ending of Philadelphia Allchorne's relationship with John Harris might have been something like as follows:

> "One possible scenario is that John was initially in a relationship with Philadelphia Allcorn and Philadelphia gave birth to Jonathan in 1800, but then John got Mary Tutt pregnant. When the child Mary was born in October 1801, she was originally recorded as Mary Tutt, but subsequently John Harris was acknowledged as the father, so the name Harris was added. As a consequence of this, the relationship between John Harris and Philadelphia Allcorn ended…."[28]

John Harris probably lived with Mary Tutt for the remainder of his life. The *1841 England Census* had them apparently living together on 6 June 1841 at Courthopes Yard, Uckfield. The Census return also noted that John was an agricultural labourer by occupation.[29] It is not known what, if any, contact Jonathan Harris had with his father and the latter's partner and daughter as Jonathan was growing up. It could well be that John Harris died in early 1845 and was buried in the churchyard of Holy Cross Church, Uckfield on 28 January 1845.[30] What ultimately became of Mary Tutt and her daughter, Mary Harris, is currently unknown.

Following the breakup of her relationship with John Harris, and with four young children, Philadelphia

---

22 See *Family Search: England, Sussex, Parish Registers,1538-1910 – Jonathan Harris* (http://tinyurl.com/y9nz9dae) (at 15 August 2020).
23 See *WikiTree – John Harris (abt. 1773-abt.1845)* (http://tinyurl.com/ycrwsmx7) (at 15 August 2020).
24 *Ibid*, at footnote 13 in the website.
25 Chiddingly is a small village around 9 km to the south-east of Uckfield. Mary Tutt was seemingly baptised in the village's Church on 15 August 1779: see *Family Search: England Births and Christenings, 1538-1975 – Mary Tutt* (http://tinyurl.com/y8mkd8n2) (at 15 August 2020). The Chiddingly Church is unusual in that it lacks a dedicatory name.
26 See *Family Search: Parish Registers and Poor Law Records for Ringmer – Mary Tutt* (http://tinyurl.com/ybg4ytt6) (at 15 August 2020).
27 See *WikiTree – Philadelphia (Newnham) Vinall (1769-1853)* (see at footnote 39, together with the accompanying text, in the website) (http://tinyurl.com/ycgz3w78) (at 15 August 2020).
28 See *WikiTree – John Harris (abt.1773-abt.1853)* (http://tinyurl.com/ycrwsmx7) (at 15 August 2020).
29 See *Ancestry – 1841 England Census for John Harris* (http://tinyurl.com/y9qp6kph) (at 15 August 2020); and *The Weald: People, History and Genealogy – John Harris, farm labourer* (http://tinyurl.com/y8dru6cw) (at 15 August 2020). Courthopes Yard was also known as "Wilson's Square". It was probably located in the west of Uckfield, where a Wilson Grove is still to be found.
30 See *SFHG: Uckfield Holy Cross 1530-1900 – John Harris* (http://tinyurl.com/y9r6vsha) (at 15 August 2020).

Allchorne would clearly have been in need of support. She found that support by marrying an Alexander Vinall in St Mary the Virgin's Church, Ringmer on 20 April 1802.[31]

Very little is presently known of Alexander Vinall's background or life. He was likely christened in St Mary the Virgin's Church, Fletching on 23 January 1780; with his parents being John and Elizabeth Vinall.[32] At the time of their marriage, Philadelphia Vinall was around 33 years of age. Her new husband was all of 22 years old. Presumably, he worked as an agricultural labourer. It is probable that Philadelphia and Alexander lived most, if not all, of their married life together in or around Buxted.

It seems that Philadelphia bore three children to Alexander Vinall. The first, Alexander Vinall Jnr, was christened in St Margaret the Queen's Church, Buxted in 1803. He grew up to be a farm labourer; marrying a Maria Pratt in St Denys' Church, Rotherfield, Sussex on 18 October 1823. Alexander and Maria Vinall appear to have had no less than 16 children together. Alexander worked for a number of years around Crowborough in Sussex before returning to Buxted in the early 1830s. He died in Buxted in 1866 aged 63 years, and was buried in the village's St Margaret the Queen's Church on 8 April 1866.[33]

Philadelphia and Alexander Vinall's second son, Edward Vinall, appears to have been born in 1806 – presumably in Buxted.[34] Virtually nothing more of Edward is presently known. However, there is a record of an Edward Vinall dying on 22 March 1880 at 1 Ropetackle, Shoreham in Sussex.[35]

The last child born to Philadelphia and Alexander was Martin Dray Vinall. Martin was born in Buxted in 1808. On 26 January 1832, he married Charity Powell in St Nicholas' Church, Brighton, Sussex. Although Martin and Charity married in Brighton, they apparently lived most of the balance of their married life in Buxted, where Martin was employed both as a grocer and as a farmer. Six children appear to have been born of the marriage. Martin Vinall died on 19 August 1876 and was buried on 23 August 1876 in the churchyard of St Margaret the Queen's Church, Buxted.[36]

Philadelphia Vinall's second husband, Alexander Vinall, died at some time between about the time of the birth of their last son in 1808 and 1834.[37] There is one website which asserts that he died at the age of 45 years at Buxted in 1825.[38] However, the primary source for this assertion is presently unknown.

Life for Philadelphia and Alexander Vinall, and for the seven children in their household, would undoubtedly have been hard. Money would have been tight. It is not presently known what level of material or personal support Alexander would have been in a position to provide to the family. As an agricultural labourer, his earnings would have been minimal at the best of times. However, particular circumstances operative in the

---

31 See *Family Search: Parish Registers and Poor Law Records for Ringmer – Alexander Vinall and Philly Alchorn* (http://tinyurl.com/yb3ro87g) (at 15 August 2020); and *Family Search: England, Sussex, Parish Registers, 1538-1910 – Alexander Vinall* (http://tinyurl.com/ybnwshgy) (at 15 August 2020).

32 See *Family Search: Parish Registers for Fletching – Alexander Vinall* (http://tinyurl.com/y9w7wh7o) (at 15 August 2020); and *Family Search: England Births and Christenings, 1538-1975 – Alexander Vinall* (http://tinyurl.com/y8hnpcnk) (at 15 August 2020). Fletching lies on the River Ouse in the Wealden District of Sussex around 4.8 km to the north-west of Uckfield. It was a major producer of bows and arrows; many of which were apparently used at the Battle of Agincourt in 1415: see *Wikipedia – Fletching, East Sussex* (http://tinyurl.com/y8a3oue7) (at 15 August 2020); and *The Weald: Town History, Bibliography and Topography – Fletching* (http://tinyurl.com/yajg6jl5) (at 15 August 2020).

33 See *The Weald: People, History and Genealogy – Alexander Vinall* (http://tinyurl.com/ycbwp4ln) (at 15 August 2020). Rotherfield is a small village located about 12 km to the north-east of Uckfield. Crowborough is a large town some 4 km to the west of Rotherfield.

34 See *The Weald: People, History and Genealogy – Edward Vinall* (http://tinyurl.com/yc4szoll) (at 15 August 2020).

35 See *England and Wales, National Probate Calendar (Index of Wills) – Vinall, Edward* (http://tinyurl.com/y93kyayk) (at 15 August 2020). Shoreham lies approximately 30 km to the south-west of Uckfield.

36 See *The Weald: People, History and Genealogy – Martin Dray Vinall* (http://tinyurl.com/y88f3blu) (at 15 August 2020); and *England and Wales, National Probate Calendar (Index of Wills) – Vinall, Martin Dray* (http://tinyurl.com/yd9tt3xd) (at 15 August 2020). Brighton is a city lying about 22 km to the south-west of Uckfield.

37 See *National Archives, Home Office, Criminal Petitions – Philadelphia Vinall* (http://tinyurl.com/yc9gocbc) (at 15 August 2020). Philadelphia is named as a widow in this 1834 Petition.

38 See *Ancestry – Alexander Vinall* (http://tinyurl.com/y97ey6de) (at 15 August 2020).

early part of the 1800s would likely have made the lives of those in the Vinall household even harder than they might otherwise have been.

In the first place, this period saw a rapid increase in England's population, coupled with increased pressure for available jobs:

> "After a period of unusual stagnation from 1700 to 1740, the population resumed its normal upward trend and afterwards between 1740 and 1780, the growth rate averaged 4 percent to 7 percent per decade, the accelerated to over 10 percent per decade until 1811. The years between 1811 and 1821 had the most rapid population growth, when it reached 17 percent per decade….
> Great Britain's population in1811 was an estimated 11 million, and by 1901 that number rapidly grew to 37 million…."[39]

The influx into Sussex of discharged soldiers and sailors after 1815 and the end of the Napoleonic Wars almost certainly exacerbated labour over-supply difficulties. As the Reverend George Gleig, of Waltham near to Canterbury in Kent, put it:

> "Multitudes of disbanded soldiers and sailors…[were] sent back to their parishes."
> This led to "a competition of men to find masters."[40]

Rural unemployment was also worsened by the introduction of new crops and new equipment, such as threshing machines, requiring less labour than manual threshing.[41]

Finally, the eruption of the Mt Tambora volcano on the Dutch East Indian island of Sumbawa in April 1815 led to havoc in England and elsewhere between that year and about 1818. The eruption was the largest in recorded history. It threw some 175 cubic km of ash and other volcanic debris, together with copious gaseous discharges, into the atmosphere, producing profound climate changes. In Europe, it caused a pronounced drop in temperatures, crop failures and famine. The year 1816, popularly referred to as "the year without a summer", saw food riots and other civil disturbances in England.[42] These could well have impacted badly on those in the Vinall household.

Like his older half-brothers, Jonathan Harris would have been required to go to work as an agricultural labourer to help support his family from a very young age. He was illiterate and clearly received no formal schooling.[43]

If the first years of the Nineteenth Century were hard ones for Philadelphia Vinall and her sons, the years

---

39 See *UK Essays: The Reasons for Rapid Population Growth in Nineteenth Century Britain* (2018) (http://tinyurl.com/yaq4no9x) (at 16 August 2020).

40 See George Gleig, *The Chronicles of Waltham* (1839), pp. 80-81. In like manner, Janet McCalman has noted that:
"The end of the Napoleonic Wars in 1815 thrust thousands into unemployment, from officers to men, triggering a crime wave that outpaced the rise in population and peaked in 1847. Crime rates rose and fell in concert with economic cycles and political unrest."
See McCalman, *op. cit.*, p.17. See also Carl J Griffin, "Parish farms and poor law: a response to unemployment in rural southern England, c. 1815-35" in (2011) 59 *Agricultural History Review* 176, 180.

41 See Christine Bean, *From Tradesman to the Poor House* (Gransden Family Website) (http://tinyurl.com/y7z2xkx4) (at 16 August 2020). See also Josie Mackie, "Social Conditions and Agriculture" in Woodchurch Ancestry Group (eds.), *Leaving Woodchurch: Emigration form Woodchurch Since the Seventeenth Century* (2011), pp. 13-14; and Griffin, *op. cit.*, at p. 177.

42 See Gillen D'Arcy Wood, *Tambora: The Eruption That Changed The World* (2014), pp. 60-62; and Wikipedia – *Year Without a Summer* (http://tinyurl.com/mkjrjap) (at 16 August 2020).

43 In 1821, Jonathan could only "make his mark", rather than sign, his Marriage Certificate: see *Family Search: Parish Registers and Poor Law Records for Mayfield- Jonathan Harris and Elizabeth Baker* (http://tinyurl.com/y3qdt88p) (at 16 August 2020).

which followed proved to be dark years, for her and for Jonathan Harris and George Allchorne, marked by crime and punishment. All three were enmeshed in crime and its consequences. The least that can be said is that Philadelphia did not set a good example for Jonathan, George and her other sons.

In July 1817, Philadelphia was tried on a charge of larceny before a judge and jury in the Court of Quarter Sessions at Lewes in Sussex. In the event, she was acquitted of the charge.[44] Less than a year later, Philadelphia was again on trial. In April or March 1818, she was tried during the Lent Assizes held in Horsham, Sussex for "uttering bad (presumably forged) money". Again, she was found to be not guilty.[45]

Taking her away from the family home for extended periods, Philadelphia Vinall's trials in 1817 and 1818, even though both resulted in acquittals, must have had a significant disruptive effect on those still living in that home. Whether Jonathan Harris was still living in the family home during these periods is not currently known. However, following his marriage in 1821 at the latest, he was certainly living elsewhere.

On 17 November 1821, Jonathan Harris married Elizabeth Baker in St Dunstan's Church, Mayfield.[46] Jonathan was 21 years old at the time of the marriage. Elizabeth was 18 years of age.

A level of controversy exists regarding Elizabeth Baker's origins and antecedents. However, an erudite and convincing analysis in a website dealing with Elizabeth concludes that she was born in 1803; the second of the six children of John Baker and the latter's wife, Sarah Baker (née Chapman).[47] Of East Sussex ancestry, John and Sarah Baker were married on 9 November 1792 in the Church of St Thomas à Becket in Framfield, Sussex.[48] Elizabeth was probably born in their home in or near to Framfield. She was baptised on 13 March 1803 in St Thomas à Becket's Church.[49]

Jonathan and Elizabeth Harris' first child, Jonathan Harris Jnr, was born in early 1822. He was christened in St Dunstan's Church, Mayfield on 10 March of that year.[50] Over the next few years, Jonathan and Elizabeth had two further children – Elizabeth Harris Jnr and Henry Harris. Neither appears to have been baptised. Elizabeth Harris Jnr was almost certainly born in 1824.[51] Henry Harris was likely born in late 1825.[52]

---

44 See *Ancestry: England and Wales, Criminal Registers 1791-1892 – Philadelphia Vinall* (http://tinyurl.com/y27wf5zy) (at 16 August 2020). The County Town of Sussex, Lewes lies about 12.5 km to the south-west of Uckfield.

45 See *Ancestry: England and Wales, Criminal Registers 1791-1892 – Philadelphia Alchorn* (http://tinyurl.com/y497tnhn) (at 16 August 2020). Horsham is a market town situated around 30 km to the north-west of Uckfield.

46 See *Family Search: Parish Registers and Poor Law Records for Mayfield – Jonathan Harris and Elizabeth Baker* (http://tinyurl.com/y3qdt88p) (at 17 August 2020). On the same day, 17 November 1821, Elizabeth's oldest sibling, Sarah Baker, married Edward Hope in the same Church: see *Family Search: Parish Registers and Poor Law Records for Mayfield – Edward Hope and Sarah Baker* (http://tinyurl.com/yyyd4hcx) (at 17 August 2020). Edward Hope was recorded as the witness to the marriage of Jonathan and Elizabeth. In turn, Jonathan was recorded as the witness to the marriage of Edward and Sarah. See also photo 1 below.

47 See *WikiTree – Elizabeth Jarvis (Baker) Harris (1802-1836)* (http://tinyurl.com/lrdxnay) (at 17 August 2020). The inclusion of "Jarvis" as a middle name for Elizabeth Harris (née Baker) in this website title is curious and unexplained. Elizabeth was clearly given only one Christian name at her baptism: see footnotes 49 and 112 below. By way of contrast, see *Ancestry: Tree – Elizabeth Baker* (http://tinyurl.com/yxr3gnml) (at 17 August 2020).

48 See *Family Search: Bishop's Transcripts of Framfield, 1662-1893 – John Baker and Sarah Chapman* (http://tinyurl.com/y3pd7snd) (at 17 August 2020).

49 See *Family Search: Parish Registers for Framfield – Elizabeth Baker* (http://tinyurl.com/y2lqmsve) (at 17 August 2020). Hadlow Down is located about 7 km to the north-east of Uckfield. It lies around 6 km to the south east of Mayfield and approximately 5 km of Framfield. Hadlow Down only became a parish in its own right in 1836: See *WikiTree – Elizabeth Jarvis (Baker) Harris (1802-1836)* (http://tinyurl.com/lrdxnay) (at 17 August 2020). John and Sarah Baker's first three children, including Elizabeth, were all baptised in Framfield. There last three children were christened in Mayfield. It seems likely that for some now unknown reason, John and Sarah switched from attending St Thomas à Becket's Church in Framfield at some stage after the birth of their third child and began attending St Dunstan's Church in Mayfield.

50 See *SFHG: Mayfield St Dunstan 1813-1836 – Jonathan Harris* (http://tinyurl.com/y5nvmx8n) (at 17 August 2020). In the Parish record of the baptism, the occupation of Jonathan Harris Snr was listed as "Labourer".

51 At the time of her passage from England to New South Wales in 1831, Elizabeth Harris Jnr was listed as being 7 years old: see *Free Passengers to NSW 1826-1837 – Elizabeth Harris* (Image 3 of 4) (http://tinyurl.com/y3wzbjm7) (at 17 August 2020). Her gravestone particulars also recorded her having been born in 1824: see *Ancestry: Australia and New Zealand, Find A Grave Index – Mrs Elizabeth Clark* (http://tinyurl.com/yyagvm6q) (at 18 August 2020).

52 See *Ancestry: Jonathan Harris Family Tree – Henry Harris* (http://tinyurl.com/y66y9rwv) (at 17 August 2020). It might be noted that in the record of Henry Harris' journey from England to New South Wales in 1831, Henry Harris was said to be two years of age: see *Free Passengers to NSW 1826-1837 – Henry Harris* (Image 4 of 4) (http://tinyurl.com/y3wzbjm7) (at 17 August 2020). This was clearly erroneous.

It would appear that for at least part of the time after his marriage to Elizabeth and prior to early 1825, Jonathan, together with Elizabeth and their first two children, were living in or about the village of Crowsborough, Sussex. Jonathan's mother, Philadelphia Vinall, and some of her other family members seem to have been living nearby during the later part of this period.[53]

It further appears that during this period from 1821 until 1825, and possibly before the period, Jonathan Harris, like his mother, had been in trouble with the law. On 3 March 1825, the *Brighton Gazette* reported that Jonathan had previously been in gaol for "fowl-stealing".[54] Particulars of the alleged offence and consequent imprisonment have not as yet been ascertained.

If Jonathan had been imprisoned for stealing poultry, as seems highly likely, then his intention in stealing the fowls may very well have been either to sell them to purchase food or to put food directly on his family's table. As an agricultural labourer in times of rural hardship, he might have been finding it very difficult to provide for himself and his family by lawful means alone or at all. And it is clears that Jonathan did not stop at stealing poultry. The worst was yet to come.

Late on the evening of Friday, 18 February 1825, or early on the morning of Saturday, 19 February 1825, at least two men broke into the home of a Mr Thomas Cobham in Uckfield. There, they stole and carried away a portable writing desk, articles of plate, wearing apparel, night linen and sundry other articles. Two men were later seen at about 3.00 am on the Saturday morning with large bundles on their backs on the road from Uckfield to Lewes.[55] Cobham subsequently offered a reward of £20 for the recovery of his property.[56]

On Monday, 28 February 1825, the *Sussex Advertiser*, which was then published weekly in Lewes, reported that:

> "On Monday (presumably, 21 February 1825), a woman named Philadelphia Vinall, and two men of the names Martin Allchin, and Jonathan Harris, alias Allchin, were apprehended in Brighton, on suspicion of being concerned in the burglary in Mr Cobham's house, at Uckfield, as stated in our last, and committed to our House of Correction for further examination before the Brighton Bench of Magistrates this day."[57]

The men arrested with Philadelphia Vinall were, of course, two of her sons: Jonathan Harris and Marin Dray Vinall. Two other men, also from Crowborough, were also implicated in the burglary. They are currently known only by their surnames – King and Homewood.[58]

---

53 See the *Brighton Gazette*, Thursday, 3 March 1825, p. 3. Crowsborough was then a village and is now a town lying some 12 km to the north-east of Uckfield, 8 km north-west of Mayfield and 6 km to the north of Hadlow Down. The town is located at the eastern margin of Ashdown Forest. The latter is today a true forest which was formerly a royal deer hunting reserve: see *The Weald: Town History, Bibliography and Topography – Ashdown Forest* (http://tinyurl.com/ya747juj) (at 18 August 2020). Prior to 1880, Crowborough lay in the Parish of Rotherfield: see *Wikipedia – Crowborough* (http://tinyurl.com/ydgh4oj3) (at 18 August 2020). Rotherfiled Parish abutted the Parish of Mayfield to the south-east and the Parish of Buxted to the south-west: see the Map of Sussex Parishes Associated with Philadelphia Newnham and her Family Members below.

54 See the *Brighton Gazette*, Thursday, 3 March 1825, p. 3.

55 See the *Sussex Advertiser*, Monday, 21 February 1825, p. 3.

56 *Ibid*.

57 See the *Sussex Advertiser*, Monday, 28 February 1825, p. 3. The Lewes House of Corrections (or the Lewes Bridewell as it was colloquially known as) was located on the corner of North and Lancaster Streets, Lewes. It replaced an earlier Lewes gaol which dated back to 1610. It opened in 1793, closed as a civil prison in 1854 and was finally demolished in 1963. The following description of it was published in 2017 by the Friends of Lewes for a Heritage Open Day:

> "It had two wings built over arcades, one for men and one for women; each of the two storeys contained 16 cells. It was enlarged to 70 cells in 1817-18, and in 1822, a treadmill was built. These were introduced into many prisons about this time, sometimes to grind corn or perform other useful tasks, but often simply as a type of hard labour....Inmates occupied small cells by night but laboured together in common work rooms during the day, when silence was rigidly enforced. Some productive work was done, or simply hard labour as a punishment".

See the Friends of Lewes, *Heritage Open Days* (http://tinyurl.com/y57ahu83) (at 19 August 2020). See also photos 2 and 3 below.

58 See footnote 59 below

It appears that although Jonathan, his mother and his half-brother were arrested in Brighton, they were soon conveyed the 12 or so km to Lewes and incarcerated in the House of Corrections to await "further examination" before Brighton Magistrates. They did not languish in the House of Corrections for long. They were soon returned to Brighton for the further examinations and a committal hearing before the Magistrates.

The examinations conducted by the Brighton Magistrates were productive. It seems that Jonathan Harris made a full confession; admitting to the burglary of Cobham's house, and also to breaking and entering into nine or ten other houses with the assistance of King and Homewood. Large quantities of apparently stolen goods were subsequently found in the houses occupied by both Philadelphia Vinall and King's father.

On Thursday, 3 March 1825, the *Brighton Gazette* wrote:

> "HOUSE-BREAKERS – JONATHAN ALLCHIN, alias HARRIS, alias VINAL, MARTIN ALLCHINN, alias VINAL, and PHILADELPHIA VINAL, their mother, were re-examined this day on the charge of burglariously entering the house of Thomas Cobham, Esq. at Uckfield, on Friday se'nnight, and Harris made a full confession, by which it appeared that he had lately broken open nine or ten different houses, assisted by two others named King and Homewood, and that on Friday se'nnight he, with King and Homewood broke open the house of Mr Cobham with a ploughshare, and took from thence the property produced. An amazing quantity of stolen goods consisting of feather beds, wearing apparel, gown pieces, &c. &c. found in the woman prisoner's and in King's father's house, was also produced by our police. The lock of Mr Cobham's desk, which we stated last week was found on the racecourse was in the woman's possession. These people lived at Crowborough, and are of notorious bad character, King, Homewood, and Harris have been in jail for fowl-stealing. King and Homewood have hitherto escaped all pursuit, although our hendboroughs have been indefatigable in their search for them, having travelled in one day upwards of sixty miles through some or the worst parts of this country. Harris is committed for trial and his mother and brother will be examined again this day."[59]

On Monday, 7 March 1825, the *Sussex Advertiser* noted that:

> "The woman and two men, who were a few days ago apprehended on suspicion of being concerned in breaking open Mr Cobham's house, at Uckfield as stated in our last, have been since examined before Magistrates in Brighton, and committed to Horsham jail, to take their trial for the offence, at the ensuing assizes. One of the above men, it is said, in the course of his examination, made a confession of several burglaries in which he had been concerned, giving, at the same time, the names of his associates, after whom the police is (sic) in active pursuit."[60]

---

59 See the *Brighton Gazette*, Thursday, 3 March 1825, p. 3. The word "se'nnight" is archaic English for a week; the space of seven days and nights: see the Merriam-Webster Dictionary – Sennight (http://tinyurl.com/ybosgt8c) (at 19 August 2020). Further, a "hendborough" in the 1820s in England was an officer with policing duties employed by a parish in lieu of a constable: see Henry Thomson, *The Military Forces and Institutions of Great Britain and Ireland (1855)* (http://tinyurl.com/ybdcsbxl) (at 19 August 2020).

60 See the *Sussex Advertiser*, Monday 7 March 1825, p. 3. The Horsham Gaol in which Jonathan, his mother and his half-brother were incarcerated was the third and last gaol constructed in that town. Its first stage was built between 1775 and 1777. According to a guide to the gaol, the first block:
"measured 126 x 32 feet and consisted of two floors over an arcaded ground floor. The debtors and felons were separated and each had 10 rooms. There were five on each side, with a five foot passageway between them. The cells were 10' 3" by 7', with a 9' high vaulted ceiling. Additionally, there was a day room measuring 28' by 12' 3". What set this Horsham prison apart from any other prison in the world, at the time, was that each prisoner had his or her own cell.… The gaol was enclosed with a 20' high wall, 18' thick.…"
See *Horsham Photography: Horsham Gaols* (http://tinyurl.com/y8hzcs3a) (at 19 August 2020). Further additions were made to the gaol over time. Be-

Following their examinations in Brighton, Jonathan Harris and his mother were each committed by one of the Magistrates, Richard Ironmonger Esq, to stand trial in Horsham during the Lent Assizes later in March 1825. Both were taken to the Horsham Gaol at Causey Croft to await their trials.

Jonathan and his mother were both tried before the Lord Chief Baron of the Court of Exchequer, Sir William Alexander, and a jury in Horsham on Wednesday, 23 March 1825. Jonathan faced two charges. The first was of:

> "burglariously breaking and entering the dwelling house of …Thomas Cobham at Uckfield and feloniously stealing therefrom six linen shifts, one mahogany desk and other articles valued at 40/- the property of Thomas Cobham."[61]

In all the Court heard evidence from 12 witnesses. One of those witnesses was Philadelphia Vinall. The nature of her evidence – including whether she testified against or on behalf of her son – is not currently known. In the event, Jonathan was found guilty of this burglary charge and sentenced to death.[62]

The charge on which Jonathan Harris was convicted was but one of some 220 which, in the early part of the Nineteenth Century, carried the death penalty in England. Most of these offences were concerned with the protection of property. The number and range of capital crimes earned this branch of the legal system the popular title of the *Bloody Code*. In 1810. A reforming Barrister and Member of Parliament, Sir Samuel Romilly, speaking in the House of Commons on capital punishment, observed that there is:

> "no country on the face of the earth in which there [have] been so many different offences according to law to be punished with death as in England."[63]

Perhaps the saving grace of the *Bloody Code* was that most of those miscreants sentenced to death in accordance with its strictures were reprieved. Between 1770 and 1830, some 35,000 death sentences were handed down in England and Wales, with around 7,000 executions actually being carried out.[64] It was to the great good fortune of Jonathan Harris, and of his descendants, that he was fated to join the majority of felons who were reprieved rather than hanged. Jonathan's sentence was commuted to transportation "for Life in a Colony Beyond the Seas".[65]

---

tween 1819 and 1822, 16 more cells were constructed, together with a large yard on the felons' side. The yard was divided into three for the use of felons, debtors and female inmates: *Ibid*. See also photo 4 below.

61 See *Ancestry: Harris, Jonathan: Trial Manuscript Notes* (http://tinyurl.com/y8aozndw) (at 19 August 2020). There is a possible indication in Jonathan Harris' Tasmanian Convict Record that Jonathan had in fact been working for Cobham at the time of the burglary. The handwritten notes on one page of the Records are not always easy to read. However, a note towards the top right of the page appears to state: "1825 Robbing my Master": see Tasmanian State Archives: *Record Books of Convicts Transported From Other Colonies and Convicted Locally* (CON 35/1/2 Image 54, p. 51) ("Jonathan Harris' Tasmanian Convict Record") (http://tinyurl.com/y8vjyu9u) (at 19 August 2020)

62 See *Ancestry: Harris, Jonathan: Trial Manuscript Notes* (http://tinyurl.com/y8aozndw) (at 19 August 2020); and *Ancestry: England and Wales, Criminal Registers, 1791-1892 – Jonathan Harris* (http://tinyurl.com/yxolnu2c) (at 19 August 2020). See also the *Sussex Advertiser*, Monday, 28 March 1825, p. 3. It is interesting to note that Martin Dray Vinall, who had originally been arrested with his mother and half-brother, appears not to have been tried during the Lent 1825 Assizes in Horsham. It will be recalled that in his confession, Jonathan Harris had implicated both King and Homewood in the breaking and entering of the Cobham and other houses: see footnote 59 and the accompanying text above. However, it appears that he did not similarly implicate his young half-brother. Given a probable lack of evidence, it seems likely that the latter was not charged with any of the burglaries. Further, the fates of King and Homewood are not presently known.

63 See Sir Samuel Romilly, *Parliamentary Debates (Hansard)*, House of Commons, Friday, 9 February 1810, cls. 366-374. See also *Wikipedia – Capital Punishment in the United Kingdom* (http://tinyurl.com/zps5zmh) (at 19 August 2020).

64 *Ibid*. Even before Jonathan Harris' trial, law reformers had begun to roll back the number of crimes which automatically carried the death penalty. Thus, the *Judgment of Death Act 1823* (UK) (4 Geo.4 c.48) gave judges the power to commute death penalties for crimes other than murder and treason: *Ibid*.

65 See *Ancestry: Harris, Jonathan: Trial Manuscript Notes* (http://tinyurl.com/y8aozndw) (at 19 August 2020).

The second charge upon which Jonathan Harris was tried was also one of burglary. He was accused of breaking and entering the home of John and Ebenezer Knight at Wivelsfield, Sussex on 24 January 1825 and stealing therefrom goods to the value of £18/13/- . On this charge, he was found not guilty.[66]

For her part, Philadelphia Vinall was charged with receiving stolen goods, convicted of the offence and sentenced to one year's imprisonment.[67] In its report of the case published on Monday, 28 March 1825, the *Sussex Advertiser* observed that she was convicted of :

> "unlawfully receiving into her possession 5 yards of printed cotton, and divers other articles, well knowing the same to have been stolen."[68]

The newspaper's account went on to state that Philadelphia was sentenced to 12 month's imprisonment in the Lewes House of Correction and also fined one shilling.[69]

Following his conviction and reprieve, Jonathan Harris was taken from Horsham to Portsmouth Harbour. On 26 April 1825, and pending transportation to New South Wales, he was taken on board the Prison Hulk *York* moored in the Harbour near Gosport.[70]

The *York*'s keel was laid down at the Nelson Dock, Rotherhithe, London in 1805. The ship was fitted out with 74 guns and launched in 1807. After active service in the Napoleonic Wars, it was decommissioned and converted into a prison ship in Portsmouth Harbour in 1819. As such, the *York* could hold up to 500 convicts in squalid conditions. The vessel was finally broken up by convicts at Woolwich in March 1854.[71]

Life for Jonathan on board the *York* would have been spartan and probably horrible. In 1826, a convict named Henry Adams made a series of complaints about his treatment on the *York*. He wrote that:

> "Convict Hulks are totally forgotten Places teeming with every Crime that can degenerate a Man."[72]

Adams complained about the cold. When he applied for a blanket, he was given a small old one. When he applied for stockings, he had to wait over two months for a pair. He wrote that:

> "nine weeks I wore a pair without washing but at length I had an old pair given to me which I could get no worsted to mend.... If I get wett I must remain in my wett cloaths, its impossible to be clean as I am now situated.... What rations I get is shamefully small."[73]

When the United Kingdom Home Office investigated Adams' complaints, the Overseer of the *York*, Alexander Lamb, responded by writing that Adams was treated the same as the other convicts. With respect to Adams' rations, Lamb wrote:

---

66 Ibid. *Wivelsfield is a small hamlet lying approximately 13.5 km to the west of Uckfield.*
67 See Ancestry: England and Wales, Criminal Registers, 1791-1892 – Philadelphia Vinall (http://tinyurl.com/y88sss2q) (at 20 August 2020).
68 See the *Sussex Advertiser*, Monday, 28 March 1825, p. 3.
69 Ibid.
70 See Ancestry: United Kingdom, Prison Hulk Registers and Letter Books, 1802-1849 (http://tinyurl.com/y2jqssch) (at 20 August 2020); and National Maritime Museum, *Prison Ship York in Portsmouth Harbour* (http://tinyurl.com/yyv4v2du) (at 20 August 2020).
71 Ibid. See also Australian National Maritime Museum, *Prison Hulk York* (http://tinyurl.com/yyhcvtsq) (at 20 August 2020); Wikipedia – *List of British Prison Hulks* (http://tinyurl.com/y56affhc) (at 20 August 2020); and photos 5, 6 and 7 below.
72 See UK National Archives Blog, 'A Floating Hell': Life on Early 19th Century Convict Hulks, p. 3 (http://tinyurl.com/y3sfgct9) (at 20 August 2020).
73 Ibid.

"His slops have been issued to him in the usual manner, bearing in mind that no new slops are issued so long as any second hand ones remain in store. He receives 3¼ oz of biscuit, three days in the week, the other three one half-penny worth of tobacco and a pint of small beer daily as a ration from the Ordnance."[74]

Notwithstanding the poor conditions endured by those on board the *York*, the convicts were put to work. They were ferried to and from the shore each working day and required to labour in the Portsmouth Naval Dockyard. In a report authored on 25 January 1825, three months before Jonathan Harris was taken on board the *York*, John Capper, the Superintendent of Ships and Vessels Employed for the Confinement of Offenders Under Sentence of Transportation, wrote:

"The Convicts confined on board the *Leviathan*, *York* and *Hardy* Hulks, in Portsmouth harbour, have been employed in carrying on Public Works under the Naval and Ordnance Boards, and the principal officers of those departments have expressed their approbation of the Prisoners' conduct when on shore executing their tasks of labour."[75]

Following their trials in Horsham in 1825, Jonathan Harris never saw his mother again. Philadelphia Vinall was taken back to Lewes to serve her 12 months imprisonment in that town's House of Corrections. Whether she served the full term or was granted early parole is not presently known. In any event, it was not to be her sole experience of gaol.

In April 1830, and aged 61 years old, Philadelphia was convicted during the Sussex Easter Quarter Sessions at Lewes of larceny. Her offence was said to have been one of "stealing flour". No details are presently available concerning the circumstances surrounding this offence; including from whom she stole the flour, how much of it she stole and why she stole it. Quite likely, impoverishment and hunger were primary motivations. It was noted in her criminal record that at the time of her conviction, she was a widow living at Maresfield.[76] In the event, her sentence was a draconian one. Because of her earlier felony conviction for receiving stolen goods, she was sentenced to be transported to the colonies for life.[77]

As matters turned out, Philadelphia avoided transportation. Following her conviction in 1830, she was conveyed from Lewes to the Horsham Gaol. Despite the Head Gaoler at that gaol assessing her character as "bad", she was classified as being "unfit for transportation". In all, it appears that she served a total of 4½ years in the gaol. In September 1834, she received a free pardon on the basis of a recommendation from Henry Tredcroft Esq, the gaol's visiting justice. Tredcroft based his recommendation on a surgeon's certificate which recorded that Philadelphia was suffering from "disease of the bladder". The grounds of the pardon granted to her were stated to be:

"Her age, her irrecoverable ill health, time served; her family will support her."[78]

---

74   See UK National Archives Blog, *'A Floating Hell': Life on Early 19th Century Convict Hulks* pp. 4-5 (http://tinyurl.com/y3sfgct9) (at 20 August 2020).

75   See the Report of John Henry Capper dated 25 January 1825 in *Accounts And Papers Of The House of Commons* (Vol. 23), p. 4 (http://tinyurl.com/y9ed467u) (at 27 August 2020); and Jen Willetts, *Free Settler or Felon: Convict Ship Marquis of Hastings 1826*, at p. 2 (http://tinyurl.com/yylr25wo) (at 27 August 2020).

76   See the *National Archives Session Rolls 179* (http://tinyurl.com/y73lnotl) (at 27 August 2020). Maresfield is a village located about 3 km to the north of Uckfield and around 3.5 km to the west of Buxted.

77   Ibid. See also *Ancestry: England and Wales, Criminal Registers, 1791-1892 for Philadelphia Vinall* (http://tinyurl.com/yamezb9c) (at 27 August 2020); and *National Archives, Home Office, Criminal Petitions – Philadelphia Vinall* (http://tinyurl.com/yc9gocbc) (at 27 August 2020).

78   See *National Archives, Home Office, Criminal Petitions – Philadelphia Vinall* (http://tinyurl.com/yc9gocbc) (at 27 August 2020).

After her release from the Horsham Gaol, Philadelphia Vinall appears to have kept out of trouble with the law and, as far as one can now tell, lived quietly for the remainder of her life. Notwithstanding her "disease of the bladder" and her "irrecoverable ill health", she live on to die in 1853 at the ripe old age of 82 years. She was buried on 4 March 1853 in the churchyard of St Margaret the Queen's Church, Buxted.[79]

By the time of Philadelphia Vinall's release from the Horsham Gaol in 1834, her second eldest son, George Allchorne (or Allcorn as he came to be known), following in the footsteps of his half-brother, Jonathan Harris, had been transported to Australia. On 10 December 1831, George found himself on trial in Lewes on a charge of receiving stolen goods. He was convicted and sentenced to be transported for seven years.[80] It has been noted that the stolen property received by George consisted of "Leather".[81] He sailed from Plymouth for good on 11 August 1832 and arrived in Hobart Town, Van Diemen's Land on 29 December 1832.[82]

And what of Elizabeth Harris, Jonathan Harris' wife, and their children? Jonathan's arrest, trial and incarceration must have had a devastating impact on them. Nothing is currently known of how they managed in the days following that arrest. It may be that Elizabeth's parents or one or more of her siblings took them in or otherwise assisted them. Alternatively, they may have sought refuge and sustenance in a local workhouse.

However, what is known is that at the time of Jonathan's arrest Elizabeth was pregnant with the couple's third child. The child, named Henry Harris by his mother, was likely born in 1825, but after his father had been gaoled.[83] The infant would have been an added burden for Elizabeth in the absence of her husband.

After some 3½ months incarcerated on the *York*, Jonathan Harris was taken from that hulk and conveyed across Portsmouth Harbour on 15 August 1825 to the convict transport ship *Marquis of Hastings*.[84] Built in London in 1819, and weighing 452 tons, the *Marquis of Hastings* was commanded by Captain William Ostler. George Rutherford was appointed as the ship's Surgeon and Superintendent of Convicts for the voyage from England to New South Wales.[85]

On 22 August 1825, the *Marquis of Hastings* sailed from Portsmouth with 152 male convicts bound for Port Jackson in New South Wales.[86] In addition to convicts and crew, the vessel carried the new Colonial Secretary for New South Wales, Alexander McLeay, together with his wife and six daughters.[87]

The *Marquis of Hastings* took 134 days before it reached Port Jackson on 3 January 1826.[88] Prior to rounding

---

79 See *SFHG: Buxted St Margaret 1567-1899* (http://tinyurl.com/yamfaf6z) 9at 27 August 2020).

80 See *Ancestry: England and Wales, Criminal Registers, 1791-1892 for George Allcorn* (http://tinyurl.com/ycf6u82n) (at 27 August 2020); *Ancestry – George Allcorn Conviction 1831* (http://tinyurl.com/y6wxv78c) (at 27 August 2020); and *Ancestry: 1831 Australian Convict Transportation Registers – George Allchorne* (http://tinyurl.com/y8fw456q) (at 27 August 2020).

81 See *Tasmanian State Archives: Alphabetical Record Book of Convicts Arriving in Van Diemen's Land, 1830-1838, "A"* (CON 31/1/2 Image 76) (http://tinyurl.com/yc9jjaz9) (at 27 August 2020).

82 *Ibid*. See also *Convict Records - George Allcorn* (http://tinyurl.com/yd55e59d) (at 27 August 2020). It is of interest to note that George Allcorn was transported to Australia on the convict ship *York*. This *York* was a different vessel from the Prison Hulk with the same name on which his half-brother, Jonathan Harris, was incarcerated in Plymouth Harbour: see *Wikipedia – York (1819 Ship)* (http://tinyurl.com/ya9hy8ns) (at 31 August 2020).

83 See footnote 57 and the accompanying text above. In 1828, and as will be seen below, Jonathan successfully petitioned to secure permission for his wife and children to join him in New South Wales. In his Petition, he referred to his unseen youngest son as "John": see *Ancestry – Harris, Jonathan 1800-1891 & Baker, Elizabeth 1802-1836 – Petition to Come to Colony* (State Records New South Wales: Colonial Secretary's Correspondence, 28/6419 – 4/1989), p.3 of 3 (http://tinyurl.com/y87ck8ub) (at 27 August 2020). Jonathan probably did not learn of the name Elizabeth had given the child until their arrival in New South Wales in 1831. See also *WikiTree – Jonathan Harris (abt. 1800-1891)* (http://tinyurl.com/ya3c6sar) (at 27 August 2020).

84 See *Ancestry: United Kingdom, Prison Hulk Registers and Letter Books, 1802-1849* (http://tinyurl.com/y2jqssch) (at 29 August 2020).

85 See *Claim A Convict: Ship Details – Marquis of Hastings (1)* (http://tinyurl.com/y6fexcdk) (at 29 August 2020); and *Wikipedia – Convict Ships to New South Wales* (http://tinyurl.com/y3vtsuym) (at 29 August 2020). See also *Convict Records – Jonathan Harris* (http://tinyurl.com/y3c8zlc6) (at 29 August 2020).

86 See *Claim A Convict: Ship Details – Marquis of Hastings (1)* (http://tinyurl.com/y6fexcdk) (at 29 August 2020).

87 See the *Sydney Gazette and New South Wales Advertiser*, Thursday, 5 January 1826, p. 2; and Willetts, *op. cit.*, at p. 5.

88 See the *Sydney Gazette and New South Wales Advertiser*, Thursday, 5 January 1926, p. 2; *Claim A Convict: Ship Details – Marquis of Hastings (1)* (http://tinyurl.com/y6fexcdk) (at 29 August 2020); and *Convict Ships to NSW 1801-1849* (http://tinyurl.com/y3vtsuym) (at 29 August 2020).

the Cape of Good Hope, it made an unscheduled stop at Rio de Janeiro in late October and early November 1825. George Rutherford, the ship's Surgeon, deemed it necessary to visit that city following an unexpectedly early outbreak of scurvy on board the vessel. In the event, there were no deaths on board during the voyage.[89]

The *Marquis of Hastings* was anchored in Sydney Harbour for six days before the convicts on board were ferried ashore. The *Sydney Gazette and New South Wales Advertiser* recorded their disembarkation and its immediate aftermath thus:

> "The male prisoners, that arrived per the Marquis of Hastings were landed on the morning of Monday last. They were not landed at the usual place in Sydney Cove, but in the Government Domain, in Farm Cove, and were then conducted to the Prisoners' Barracks in Hyde Park. His Excellency the GOVERNOR in CHIEF inspected these men in the barrack-yard; and was pleased to hold out to them the prospect of every encouragement, on condition of exemplary behaviour; after which they were distributed throughout the Country. The majority were forwarded to the interior by water, for the purpose of accommodating the settlers, who have been so badly off for labourers for a considerable time past."[90]

An indent for the convicts arriving in Sydney in 1826 on board the *Marquis of Hastings* provides a description of Jonathan Harris at that time. He was recorded as being 25 years old, 5′ 6″ in height, of fair complexion and with blue eyes and brown hair.[91]

It appears that Jonathan did not remain long at the Prisoners' Barracks in Hyde Park. Like the majority of the other convicts from the *Marquis of Hastings*, he was quickly assigned to work for a settler. The Indent for the *Marquis of Hastings* convicts noted that he was "disposed of" to "Mr. Thompson South Creek".[92] The "Mr Thompson" referred to in the Indent was in fact Charles Tompson of South Creek.

Charles Tompson was born in Birmingham, England in 1784. In March 1802, he was convicted at the Warwick Assizes of stealing two books and sentenced to be transported to the colonies for seven years. He arrived in Sydney in 1804. Being literate, he was almost immediately assigned to work as a clerk in the Office of the New South Wales Commissary, John Palmer. Upon the completion of his sentence in 1811, Tompson set up shops in Pitt and Hunter Streets, Sydney from which he sold provisions to ships in Sydney Harbour.

In 1819, Tompson purchased a 700 acre (approximately 283 hectares) farming property on the Richmond

---

89 As the following extract from George Rutherford's Journal for the voyage makes clear, Jonathan Harris and the other convicts on board the *Marquis of Hastings* were indeed fortunate to have as competent a surgeon as Rutherford in charge of their welfare during their transportation to Australia:
"I beg most respectfully to observe [that] the few cases of acute diseases which occurred in the course of the voyage may be ascribed to the favourable season of the year in which we sailed, having left in the latter end of August when fine weather was to be expected off the Cape of Good Hope, and during the remainder of the passage. On no former occasion, however, did scurvy make its appearance so early as on this present, having manifested symptoms before we reached the Line [the Equator]. Knowing from the experience of former voyages what I had to expect by entering the wet and cold southern latitudes before reaching the Cape, I considered it advisable to put into Rio [de] Janeiro for refreshments. Little else could be done than arresting the progress of the disease when it made its appearance up to that date by the usual means: liberating men from irons and obliging them to take exercise, keeping the prison clean, dry and truly ventilated, administering lime juice in such quantity as they could bear without affecting the stomach or bowels. Diarrhoea on this occasion as on all others was found most frequent and troublesome, particularly soon after the ship passed the Line.... I had no deaths on board....[N]o symptom of scurvy manifested itself after leaving Rio [de] Janeiro"
See George Rutherford, "Journal of the Convict Ship Marquis of Hastings: 2 July 1825 to 9 January 1826" in *UK, Royal Naval Medical Journals, 1817-1856*, at pp. 18-19 (http://tinyurl.com/yyzfvlga) (at 29 August 2020). See also Willetts, *op. cit.*, at pp. 3-4.
90 See the *Sydney Gazette and New South Wales Advertiser*, Thursday, 12 January 1826, p. 3. The Governor who addressed the convicts was General Ralph Darling. The Prisoners' Barracks in Hyde Park is today better known as the *Hyde Park Barracks*. See also Willetts, *op. cit.*, pp. 5-6; and photos 8 and 9 below.
91 See *New South Wales Convict Indents, 1788-1842 for Jonathan Harris* (http://tinyurl.com/y5jonf9h) and (http://tinyurl.com/y68vy9dc) (both at 32 August 2020)
92 *Ibid.*

Road in what is now Marsden Park on the north-western outskirts of Sydney. Having acquired a further 1,000 acres (around 405 hectares) of adjacent land, he had by 1825 constructed a two storey brick dwelling on the enlarged property. The house faced the South Creek. Tompson called his home *Clydesdale*.[93] It was to *Clydesdale* that Jonathan Harris was sent in January 1826.

Jonathan's time at *Clydesdale* was fruitful and productive, both for him and for Tompson. His labouring duties on the property were no doubt similar to those he had been employed to perform since his young days in East Sussex. In the *1828 New South Wales Census*, he was listed as one of four labourers among the servants working on the property.[94] Over time, it would appear that Jonathan engendered both the friendship and support of his master.

On 21 July 1828, Jonathan forwarded a Petition to the Governor, General Ralph Darling requesting that the Governor recommend to the Secretary of State for the Colonies that Jonathan's wife and children be sent at Government expense to join him in New South Wales.[95] As can be seen from his endorsement on it, the Petition had the full support of Charles Tompson. It may well have been drawn up and lodged at his instigation. The Petition was duly dispatched by the Governor to the Colonial Office in London, where permission for the reuniting voyage was in time granted.[96]

Elizabeth Harris and her three children departed London for New South Wales on 8 July 1830 as free passengers on board the *Kains*. The *Kains* was a vessel of 353 tons under the command of Captain William Goodwin. In addition to the Harris family members and a number of other free or paying passengers, it carried 118 female convicts.[97]

On board the *Kains* on its voyage to Sydney was a young seaman named Charles Picknell. Unlike the relatively quick journey of the *Marquis of Hastings*, that of the *Kains* lasted all of eight months. Picknell kept a diary of the trip up until the *Kains* reached Cape Town on 23 November 1830. If Jonathan Harris' journey to New South Wales under the enlightened supervision of Surgeon Rutherford had been largely uneventful apart from the scourge of scurvy, that of his wife and children was anything but uneventful. Not only was the *Kains* also afflicted with scurvy, but it was the setting for mutinies, an averted threat from a suspected Spanish pirate ship, drunkenness and the death of a number of female convicts and children of convicts.[98]

Charles Picknell mentioned Elizabeth Harris in his diary twice. He noted that:

"On the 6th [of July 1830] three free women named White, Arthur and Harris came aboard."[99]

Picknell also recorded that in November 1830, Captain Goodwin accused him of "talking to Mrs Harris, one of the three free women on board".[100]

---

93 See *Convict Records – Charles Tompson* (http://tinyurl.com/yxhzqwe5) (at 31 August 2020); The 1788-1820 Pioneer Association, *The People in the Life and Times of Lachlan and Elizabeth Macquarie – Charles Tompson* (http://tinyurl.com/yyyaiqpu) (at 31 August 2020); and *Wikipedia – Clydesdale, Marsden Park* (http://tinyurl.com/y2wcmr5c) (at 31 August 2020). See also photo 10 below.

94 See *Ancestry – 1828 New South Wales Census for Jonathan Harris* (http://tinyurl.com/y9gnyquo) (at 31 August 2020).

95 See *Ancestry – Harris, Jonathan 1800-1891 & Baker, Elizabeth 1802-1836 – Petition to Come to Colony* (State Records New South Wales: Colonial Secretary's Correspondence, 26/6419 – 4/1989) (Image 3 of 3) (http://tinyurl.com/be3se3fh) (at 31 August 2020).

96 Ibid.

97 See *Free Passengers to NSW 1826-1837* (Images 1-4) (http://tinyurl.com/y3wzbjm7) (at 31 August 2020); *Claim a Convict: Ship Details – Kains* (http://tinyurl.com/yy4zy86a) (at 31 August 2020); *Convict Records – Kains Convict Ship* (http://tinyurl.com/y5l4eusa) (at 31 August 2020); and *Wikipedia – Convict Ships to New South Wales* (http://tinyurl.com/y3vtsuym) (at 31 August 2020).

98 See the *Sydney Morning Herald*, Saturday, 10 May 1930, p. 11; the *Sydney Morning Herald*, Saturday, 17 May 1930, p. 11; and the *Sydney Morning Herald*, Saturday, 24 May 1930, p. 11.

99 See the *Sydney Morning Herald*, Saturday, 10 May 1930, p. 11.

100 See the *Sydney Morning Herald*, Saturday, 24 May 1930, p. 11.

The *Kains* finally anchored at Port Jackson on 11 March 1831.[101] Fortunately, Elizabeth Harris and her three children all arrived safely. Soon afterwards, they were united with Jonathan. On *Clydesdale*, the Harris family would have lived in one of the small dwelling huts, each constructed of wood, which surrounded the mansion house.

In early 1831, the Harris family were still living at *Clydesdale* and Jonathan was still working as a labourer under assignment to Charles Tompson. However, in late March of that year, Elizabeth Harris applied by Petition to Governor Darling requesting either that Jonathan be re-assigned to her or that a Ticket of Exemption from Government Labour be granted to him.[102]

The contents of Elizabeth Harris' Petition are interesting in that they serve to throw further light on the family's circumstances (and particularly those of Jonathan Harris) at and prior to the time the Petition was forward to the Governor. Leaving aside formalities, it reads:

"That your Petitioner arrived in the Colony on the ship Kains with three small children under the sanction of the British Government to join her husband Jonathan Harris, per ship Marquis of Hastings (1), who is a prisoner for life in the assigned service of Mr. C. Tompson of South Creek, with whom he has been upwards of five years.

That her husband possesses about twelve head of horned cattle, principally females, partly the offspring of two cows and calves, the bounty of his Master as a reward for extraordinary good conduct, and partly the savings of his own industry at nights in making straw hats – which cattle are by permission now depasturing with his Master's herd.

That your Petitioner, deeply impressed with gratitude for the great boon that has been granted to her and her children in being permitted to rejoin her husband and their father, yet ventures to approach your Excellency to state that it is her intention to rent and cultivate a small farm for the support of her family, provided your Excellency will be graciously pleased to allow her husband (who is bred to farming pursuits) to labour for the support of his family either by assignment to your Petitioner or under a Ticket of Exemption."[103]

Elizabeth was supported (and almost certainly encouraged) in her Petition by Charles Tompson. Tompson favourably endorsed the document in no uncertain terms as follows:

---

101 See *Convict Records – Kains Convict Ship* (http://tinyurl.com/y5l4eusa) (at 31 August 2020).
102 On 1 January 1830, the Colonial Secretary's Office in Sydney sent a circular to all Magistrates in the Colony outlining the differences between "the several forms of remission of sentence granted to prisoners of the Crown". The circular advised that a Ticket of Leave:
"is permission to an individual to employ himself for his own benefit, and to acquire property, on condition of residing within the district therein specified; of presenting himself and producing his Ticket before the Magistrates at the periods prescribed by the regulations; and of attending Divine Service weekly if performed within a reasonable distance. But he is not allowed to remove to another district without the express sanction of Government entered on the face of his Ticket: the Ticket itself is liable to be resumed at any time at the pleasure of the Governor, and, in that case, the individual reverts to the situation of a prisoner of the Crown in every respect."
The circular went on to state that a Ticket of Exemption from Government Labour:
"differs from a Ticket of Leave, in conferring no permission for the individual to employ himself for his own benefit, or to acquire property, but simply the privilege of residing until the next 31st December, with the person therein named, generally a relation, in some specific district, and no other. In requiring the attendance at Muster and Divine Worship, it is as strict as a Ticket of Leave, and, like it, is liable to resumed at any time by His Excellency's order; it is also void, if not renewed on the 1st of January, every year, and the holder then becomes liable to be treated as a prisoner of the Crown, unlawfully at large."
See *Claim a Convict – Ticket of Leave Regulations* (http://tinyurl.com/yawgmp4j) (at 31 August 2020). See also NSW State Archives & Records, *Convict Tickets of Exemption from Government Labour* (http://tinyurl.com/ycpq5p6t) (at 31 August 2020).
103 See *Ancestry – Baker, Elizabeth 1802-1836 – Petition to have Jonathan Assigned* (http://tinyurl.com/ycuds3wa) (at 31 August 2020).

"I respectfully beg leave to certify for the information of His Excellency the Governor that Jonathan Harris, the husband of the Petitioner, has been in the Colony upwards of five (5) years, and that he has been in my service the whole of that time. His conduct has been remarkably sober and industrious and I have no doubt of his entire willingness and ability to maintain and bring up his family in a decent and comfortable manner. All that the Petitioner has stated respecting the cattle and other matters is strictly true."[104]

On 14 May 1831, Frederick Hely, the Principal Superintendent of Convicts for New South Wales, approved the grant of a Ticket of Exemption from Government Labour to Jonathan Harris in response to Elizabeth' Petition.[105] The Ticket which issued was dated 1 June 1831. It permitted Jonathan to live with Elizabeth in the Windsor District.[106] At the time, the Windsor District encompassed *Clydesdale*.

Following the issue to Jonathan of the Ticket of Exemption from Government Labour, it may be that Elizabeth was able to lease, or secure a licence to use, land proximate to *Clydesdale*. Alternatively, Charles Tompson may have provided her with either a lease or a licence for part of the *Clydesdale* lands. However, it is arguably more likely that Jonathan, Elizabeth and their children continued to live on *Clydesdale*, with Jonathan continuing to work for Tompson as before, while Jonathan searched for alternative accommodation and possibly employment.

It would seem that towards the end of 1831, the Harris family obtained alternative accommodation, not in the Windsor District but in the neighbouring Parramatta District. On 2 January 1832, Jonathan was issued with a replacement Ticket of Exemption from Government Labour which entitled him to live with Elizabeth in the latter District.[107] Where they lived in the Parramatta District is not currently known. Elizabeth was probably able to secure occupancy of a small allotment on which the family lived, with Jonathan labouring for the allotment's owner or a neighbouring landholder.

The Harris family did not remain long in the Parramatta District. A note endorsed on the Ticket of Exemption from Government Labour issued to Jonathan on 2 January 1832 stated:

"To be received for Argyle vide letter from Parramatta 19 January 1833."[108]

Although somewhat cryptic, this note suggests that by 19 January 1833, Jonathan and Elizabeth were planning to move from the Parramatta District to the Argyle District. What is clear, however, is that the 1832 Ticket granted to Jonathan was the last of such Tickets he received. In August 1833, he was formally assigned by the Colonial Government to work for his wife Elizabeth.[109]

It is also clear that Jonathan and Elizabeth Harris had three further children together in New South Wales. Their first such child, Sophia Harris, was born on 15 January 1832 and baptised on 26 January of that year.[110] Their next child, Thomas Harris, was born on 28 December 1833 and baptised on 13 July 1834.[111] Their last child,

---

104 *Ibid.*

105 *Ibid* (see p. 1 of 4).

106 See *Ancestry – Exemption from Government Labour for Jonathan Harris, 1831* (http://tinyurl.com/yxjkom6l) (at 1 September 2020). See also *NSW State Records – Convict Index for Jonathan Harris* (http://tinyurl.com/y5c2hlqt) (at 1 September 2020).

107 See *Ancestry – Approved Ticket of Exemption Location Transfer Application for Jonathan Harris, September 1831* (http://tinyurl.com/ybn6mmhr) (at 1 September 2020); and *Ancestry – Exemption from Government Labour for Jonathan Harris, 1832* (http://tinyurl.com/y6t2pwyh) (at 1 September 2020). See also *NSW State Records – Convict Index for Jonathan Harris* (http://tinyurl.com/y5c2hlqt) (at 1 September 2020).

108 See *Ancestry – Exemption from Government Labour for Jonathan Harris, 1832* (http://tinyurl.com/y6t2pwyh) (at 2 September 2020).

109 See *NSW State Records – Convict Index for Jonathan Harris* (http://tinyurl.com/y5c2hlqt) (at 2 September 2020).

110 See *Ancestry – St John's Church, Parramatta Baptism Record for Sophia Harris* (http://tinyurl.com/y2qxbc3q) (at 2 September 2020).

111 See *Ancestry – St John's Church, Parramatta Baptism Record for Thomas Harris* (http://tinyurl.com/y4a9fcn7) (at 2 September 2020).

George Jarvis Harris, was born on 19 August 1835 and baptised on 9 December 1835.[112] All three children were christened in St John's Church, Parramatta.

At some point in time between Thomas' christening on 13 July 1834 and George's christening on 9 December 1835, the Harris family made their move from the Parramatta District to the Argyle District. In the Baptism Records of St John's Church, Parramatta, Jonathan was said to have had his abode in Parramatta and to have been employed as a labourer when Thomas was baptised.[113] In contrast, the Church's Baptism Records note that Jonathan was living on the Goulburn Plains and working as a farmer at the time of George's baptism.[114]

It seems highly likely that when Jonathan, Elizabeth and their children shifted from the Parramatta District to the Argyle District, they moved directly on to land owned by William Shelley. In a letter written by Major Edmund Lockyer through the New South Wales Colonial Secretary to the Governor on 28 December 1842, Lockyer wrote of Jonathan:

> "In 1835, he was in the employ of William Shelley Esquire of Argyle, now a Magistrate, and occupied a small portion of land of that gentleman adjoining my Estate of Lockyersleigh in Argyle."[115]

William Shelley, the son of a Congregational Church missionary and trader, was born in Sydney in 1803. His brother, George Shelley, was born in 1812. The two brothers were pioneer squatters in the Tumut River valley, first taking cattle there in 1829. They initially established the *Bombowlee* run of 27,000 acres (approximately 10,927 hectares) at the junction of the Tumut River with the Gilmore Creek in 1829. Then in 1839, they acquired the *Tumut Plains* run of 20,000 (about hectares 8,094 acres) immediately to the south of *Bombowlee*.[116]

---

112 See *Ancestry – St John's Church, Parramatta Baptism Record for George Jarvis Harris* (http://tinyurl.com/y6c63h7t) (at 2 September 2020). It is interesting to note that George Jarvis Harris was the only one of Jonathan and Elizabeth's six children to be baptised with a middle name. In her unpublished biography of Jonathan Harris, Margaret Cooper wrote:

"The choice of 'Jarvis' as a second name for [Jonathan's] newborn son was interesting. The Antill family holdings were called 'Jarvisfield' after Macquarie's first wife; Major Antill being a friend and aide-de-camp to Macquarie. Major Antill's son, H. C. Antill, performed the burial of Elizabeth at Red Bank Stone Quarry."

See Margaret Cooper, *Biography of Jonathan Harris* (http://tinyurl.com/ycuhrduv) (at 2 September 2020). Major Henry Colden Antill arrived in Sydney with Governor Lachlan Macquarie in December 1809. On 1 January 1810, he was appointed an aide-de-camp to Macquarie. Retiring from the British Army in 1821, he received a grant of 2,000 acres (about 809 hectares) at what was then known as Stonequarry and is now Picton. In due course, he named the property *Jarvisfield* as a tribute to Macquarie's first wife, Jane Macquarie, whose maiden surname was Jarvis. Major Antill served as a Police Magistrate from 1829 until his death in 1852: see *Wikipedia – Jarvisfield, Picton* (http://tinyurl.com/y4gbjzgs) (at 2 September 2020). He both reported Elizabeth Harris' death to the New South Wales Colonial Secretary in 1836: see *Ancestry – Letter from Henry Antill to the Colonial Secretary dated 1 April 1836* (http://tinyurl.com/y66t4pdt) (at 5 September 2020); and conducted a funeral service for her at Cobbitty on 3 April 1836: see *Ancestry – Baker, Elizabeth 1802-1836: Narrellan Burial Record* (http://tinyurl.com/yylokygt) (at 5 September 2020). If Jonathan and Elizabeth Harris were inspired by Major Antill's *Jarvisfield* to give their son George the middle name of Jarvis, then the reason for them taking that step is unknown. However, it is possible that shortly prior to George's birth, Major Antill, in his capacity as a Police Magistrate or otherwise, performed a service or an act of kindness to a member or members of the Harris family. See also footnote 47 above.

113 See *Ancestry – St John's Church, Parramatta Baptism Record for Thomas Harris* (http://tinyurl.com/y4a9fcn7) (at 3 September 2020).

114 See *Ancestry – St John's Church, Parramatta Baptism Record for George Jarvis Harris* (http://tinyurl.com/y6c63h7t) (at 3 September 2020).

115 See *Ancestry – Letter from Edmund Lockyer to the Colonial Secretary dated 28 December 1842* (http://tinyurl.com/y7k5dqxp) (at 3 September 2020) ("the *Lockyer Letter*"). A complete transcription of the *Lockyer Letter* is appended below.

Edmund Lockyer was born in Devon, England in 1784. Joining the British Army, he rose to the rank of major. With a detachment of troops, he arrived in Sydney in 1825. In August of that year, he explored the Brisbane River at the direction of the New South Wales Governor, Sir Thomas Brisbane. In 1826, the new Governor, General Ralph Darling, instructed Lockyer to examine King George Sound in what became Western Australia with a view to the possible establishment of a British settlement. In 1827, he left the Army and was granted 2,560 acres (around 1,036 hectares) on what was then known as the Goulburn Plains near present-day Marulan. Gradually increasing the extent of this holding, Lockyer came to call it *Lockyersleigh*. He acquired other lands in New South Wales over time, including a house, *Ermington*, near Ryde. He subsequently received a number of government appointments, including that of a Police Magistrate at Parramatta: see Anon., "Lockyer, Edmund (1784-1860)" in *Australian Dictionary of Biography* (http://tinyurl.com/yykltj6g) (at 3 September 2020); *Wikipedia – Edmund Lockyer* (http://tinyurl.com/yxfvuknp) (at 3 September 2020); and *Trove: Lockyersleigh Homestead, Marulan* (http://tinyurl.com/y3s4sf2x) (at 3 September 2020).

Perhaps with significant justification, Lockyer nursed a grudge against Jonathan Harris. His evident purpose with the *Lockyer Letter* was to persuade the Colonial Government not to mitigate a sentence of transportation for 15 years to a penal settlement which, as will be seen below, was imposed on Jonathan on 10 September 1842: see the *Lockyer Letter* (http://tinyurl.com/y7k5dqxp) (at 3 September 2020). See also photo 11 below.

116 See Neil Gunson, "Shelley, William James (1774-1815)" in *Australian Dictionary of Biography* (http://tinyurl.com/y3vbrx8x) (at 3 September 2020);

At some time prior to 1835, William Shelley apparently acquired land in his own right adjacent to Lockyer's *Lockyersleigh* property. Shelley's land was located on the Goulburn Plains some 20 km to the north-east of Goulburn and extended into a low range of hills then known as the Grampian Hills. It lay to the east of Towrang and to the west of Brayton. It seems likely that Shelley called his property *Grampian Hills*. The portion of the land occupied by the Harris family abutted Lockyersleigh immediately to its north.[117]

It would seem that Jonathan Harris established a good relationship with William Shelley. Jonathan was apparently employed to work both on the latter's *Grampian Hills* property and on the Shelley brothers' Tumut River valley runs. It would also seem that the Harris family both grew produce for home consumption and for sale and grazed Jonathan's cattle on the land that Shelley allowed them to occupy.

Soon after entering William Shelley's employ and occupying part of his *Grampian Hills* land, it could well be that Jonathan lapsed back into old dishonest ways. That was certainly Edmund Lockyer's view. In the *Lockyer Letter*, Lockyer wrote that shortly after Jonathan had begun residing on Shelley's property:

> "I was plundered of a large quantity of wheat, and having heard that Jonathan Harris had sold wheat to various persons, and well knowing he had none to reap, great suspicion was attached to him at the time that he was the party who stole my wheat.
>
> I had stolen about the same time the iron axle of a dray with the wheels from off the body of a dray that was left in one of my paddocks, distant about a mile from Harris's hut. I went my self to his residence and informed him of the robbery, and whilst talking to him, I observed he repeatedly looked to a place called the Sandy Creek (possibly now known as the Narambulla Creek) that caused me to suspect it was secreted there. I went to my establishment and returned accompanied by my overseer, a Mr Graham, and two of my servants to the Sandy Creek, and after two hours or more search we found the axle and the wheels buried in the sand. This left no doubt in my mind he was the thief or was accessory to the removal, though this would not have been sufficient even to have taken him for summary jurisdiction. I, however, complained and stated these circumstances to Mr Shelley: when he admitted the strong suspicions against Harris, still retained him and employed him conveying supplies from his residence at the Grampian Hills in Argyle to his station on the Tumut River."[118]

Jonathan Harris and his children must have been left distraught on 30 March 1836 when Elizabeth Harris was killed in a tragic accident. Perhaps the best available description of the circumstances surrounding this accident is to be found in a report of it published in the *Sydney Gazette and New South Wales Advertiser* on 2 April 1836 in the following terms:

> "DREADFUL ACCIDENT — On Wednesday last, as a cart containing a woman and infant child, driven by a lad the son of the woman, was proceeding from Bong Bong to Campbelltown on the way to the market, the lad allowed the horse to swerve from the road, and coming on a ridge capsized it, when awful to relate, the woman fell under the cart, and was crushed to death; the feelings of the lad, who was unable

---

John Stephenson, *The Beautiful Blowering Valley – Bombowlee* (http://tinyurl.com/y55973sn) (at 3 September 2020); and John Stephenson, *The Beautiful Blowering Valley – Tumut Plains Run* (http://tinyurl.com/y80xbey6) (at 3 September 2020).

117   See the Goulburn Plains Plan below.
118   See the *Lockyer Letter* (http://tinyurl.com/y7k5dqxp) (at 4 September 2020).

to raise the cart from off his dying parent can be better imagined than portrayed. Sometimes after, the mail passing, rendered all the assistance possible, but the hand of death had marked the unfortunate women for his victim; all aid was in vain; the child, strange to say, escaped uninjured. A coroner's inquest was convened at the time our informant left Campbelltown, the result of which we are not aware of."[119]

In a letter sent to the Colonial Secretary, Alexander Macleay, for the attention of the Governor, Sir Richard Bourke, Henry Antill, of *Jarvisfield*, had earlier written on 1 April 1836 of Elizabeth's death, and had also complained of the state of the road where she died. Antill stated in his letter that:

"I have the honour to report for the information of His Excellency the Governor that on Wednesday morning last a woman of the name of Elizabeth Harris free, wife I understand of a Ticket of Leave holder residing near Mr Shelley's farm on the Goulburn road, met her death by the overturning of her cart on the road between this and Myrtle Creek. She had a young baby in her arms who Providentially escaped unhurt. She has left a husband and five Children and joined him from England about five years back.

I would beg leave to take this opportunity to call His Excellency's attention to the bad state of the road where this accident happened. It is but a short distance but I consider it a part of the Argyle Road that requires the most repair."[120]

Apparently, Antill's complaint regarding the road received short shrift from either the Colonial Secretary or the Governor, one of whom on 21 April 1836 noted on Antill's letter:

"The event related by the Magistrate is a very melancholy one — but I know the road and do not consider it more dangerous than very many others now are and must continue to be on basis of great extent and little or no population."[121]

The lad driving Elizabeth's cart when it overturned was probably her oldest son, Jonathan Harris Jnr, who would then have been 14 years of age. However, it is possible that the driver was her second son, Henry Harris. Henry would have been 11 years of age at the time of the accident, and was likely well-versed in driving the horse and cart. Without much doubt, the infant thrown clear from Elizabeth's arms during the accident would have been George Jarvis Harris. George was eight months old at the time.

It is not now known precisely where the accident took place. However, it was clearly on part of what was then known as the Argyle or Goulburn Road, and more recently as the Old Hume Highway. It probably occurred somewhere between what is now Picton (until 1841 called Stonequarry) and Campbelltown. It would seem that

---

119   See the *Sydney Gazette and New South Wales Advertiser*, Saturday, 2 April 1836, p. 2.
120   See Ancestry – Baker, Elizabeth 1802-1836: Death Report by H. C. Antill (http://tinyurl.com/ycuclxxl) (at 4 September 2020). See also footnote 112 above. Henry Antill's concern regarding the state of the road where Elizabeth Harris was killed was echoed in a subsequent, if somewhat garbled, report of the accident published in the *Sydney Herald* on 21 April 1836:
   "THE ROADS – the road between Myrtle Creek and the Stonequarry has long been in so bad a state as to be almost impassable for the market carts and teams from the New Country. Last week Mrs. Harris of Parramatta, who was returning from Argyle, was thrown from a cart which was upset by the wheel passing into a deep rut in the road, and killed on the spot. The report of the Inquest has not reached town, but it is to be hoped that a Jury will make such a representation to the Government as to cause an enquiry into the case, and repairs of the road."
   See the *Sydney Herald*, Thursday, 21 April 1836, p. 2.
121   See Ancestry – Baker, Elizabeth 1802-1836: Death Report by H. C. Antill (http://tinyurl.com/ycuclxxl) (at 4 September 2020).

Elizabeth and her children were en route to the Campbellfield market from their land on *Grampian Hills* to sell family produce.

Elizabeth Harris' funeral was conducted on 3 April 1836 by Henry Antill at Cobbitty in the Parish of Narrellan, a short distance to the north-west of Campbellfield. Her death was also registered in Cobbitty.[122] She was almost certainly buried in an unmarked grave in an area then and now known as Redbank, located on the southern outskirts of present day Picton to the south-west of Cobbitty.[123]

Elizabeth's death would have had a devastating impact on Jonathan Harris and his children. In addition to the emotional trauma which must have resulted, her passing would have deprived the family of her practical support. How Jonathan coped is not now known. However, he must have relied to a very significant extent on his two eldest children, Jonathan Harris Jnr and, in particular, Elizabeth Harris Jnr, in caring for the younger children.

It would seem that shortly after Elizabeth's death, Jonathan moved with his children from their home on the *Grampian Hills* property to the Shelley brothers' *Bombowlee* run on the Tumut River.[124] It may be that he felt that the children could be better cared for on *Bombowlee*.

It is also unclear what effect Elizabeth's death had on Jonathan's legal status. In Elizabeth's Narrellan Parish Burial Record, she was described as having been the wife of a Ticket of Leave holder.[125] If accurate, this would mean that Jonathan had been granted a Ticket of Leave (probably with Henry Antill's support) at some point in time between his assignment in August 1833 to work for Elizabeth and the latter's death in March 1836. However, no such Ticket of Leave has come to light to date.

If, contrary to the indication in Elizabeth's Narrellan Parish Burial Record, Jonathan had not been granted a Ticket of Leave prior to her death, then two possibilities logically remain. He may have been re-assigned by the Colonial Government after that death to work for some other free person. If so, the most likely such person would have been William Shelley. However, again, no record of such a re-assignment has been unearthed to date. The second possibility is that Jonathan somehow "slipped through the net"; continuing to work for Shelley, and to live with his children on Shelley's property, without being assigned to him or possessing a Ticket of Leave. This would have left Jonathan living outside the law.

Very shortly after Elizabeth's death, Jonathan was again accused of theft by Edmund Lockyer. In the *Lockyer Letter*, Lockyer wrote the following account of the alleged theft and its aftermath:

> "In April 1836, I sent a herd of cattle in charge of a young man, an emigrant, a Mr John Stroud, to a place called Mingay on the Murrumbidgee River. On his route between Yass and that place, he met Jonathan

---

122 See *Ancestry – Baker, Elizabeth 1802-1836: Narrellan Burial Records* (http://tinyurl.com/yylokygt) (at 5 September 2020); and *Ancestry – New South Wales Births, Deaths and Marriages; Burials – Elizabeth Harris* (http://tinyurl.com/y3w3wumm) (at 5 September 2020). See also *Ancestry – Australian Death Index, 1787-1985: Elizabeth Harris* (http://tinyurl.com/y5pbcqzf) (at 5 September 2020).

123 See *WikiTree – Elizabeth Jarvis (Baker) Harris (1802-1836)* (http://tinyurl.com/lrdxnay) (at 5 September 2020). In writing of the history of Picton, Liz Vincent observed that:
"The area for a government town, just south of the Picton we know today was first set aside in November 1821. The area is now known as Upper Picton or Redbank. It is on the Redbank Reserve, its southern boundary Redbank Creek, Stonequarry Creek on the east, Prince Street on the north side and Rumker Street on its western side"
See Liz Vincent, *Internet Family History Association of Australia: Picton NSW – The Early Years* (http://tinyurl.com/yxsj9nyx) (at 5 September 2020). Although there are currently two cemeteries in the Redbank area, there would seem to be no record of Elizabeth's grave lying within the bounds of either of them.

124 See the *Lockyer Letter* (http://tinyurl.com/y7k5dqxp) (at 5 September 2020). See also footnote 116 and the accompanying text above.

125 See *Ancestry – Baker, Elizabeth 1802-1836: Narrellan Burial Records* (http://tinyurl.com/yylokygt) (at 5 September 2020).

Harris driving a team of bullocks with a dray, when Stroud observed he had three of my working bullocks yoked to his team. He asked Harris how he had come by them, where he replied they had been lent to his son by one of my men at Lockyersleigh. Stroud told him that could not be true as no one could lend him my bullocks except my self or overseer, and therefore he must have stolen them, and asked him to unyoke them. Stroud took possession of the bullocks and drove them to Mingay with the herd of cattle.

On this being represented to me, I applied to the Bench at Goulburn to have Harris brought before it for the stealing of my bullocks, but most extraordinarily, and though a prisoner of the Crown and living on Mr Shelley's station on the Tumut, he was not taken into custody until ten months afterwards, and only then on my offering a reward of five pounds which I paid when brought to Goulburn, where he was committed to take his trial at the Supreme Court, Sydney for cattle stealing and was tried before Mr Justice Burton and acquitted from my inability to prove felonious intent owing to the non-appearance of the principal evidence, Mr Stroud, who, in September 1836, had been found drowned in the Jugiong Creek near Yass.[126] His Honour Mr [Justice] Burton, in addressing Harris, said the case had failed, still he had heard quite enough to be satisfied that he was a bad character, and directed that the Clerk of the Court should write a letter to the Principal Superintendent of Convicts to receive Jonathan Harris into Government [charge], and that he was of no account again to be assigned or have any indulgences. Owing, I presume, to His Honour going to England shortly after this man's trial, or omission of the Clerk of the Court, Harris obtained his Ticket of Leave in less than a month after his trial and returned to his old residence and employ at Mr Shelley's at the Grampian Hills where he set up and drove about in his gig."[127]

Lockyer followed his observations in the *Lockyer Letter* on Jonathan Harris' 1837 trial with the following remarks regarding the circumstances surrounding the drowning of John Stroud:

"The circumstances attending the death of Mr Stroud were very suspicious as he was a young man of excellent moral character. He had left Yass on the morning of his death and called at a house of refreshment at Bogolong or near it, no public house at that time being beyond Yass, and asked a woman to give him breakfast, and asked her at the same time if she could change a one pound note as otherwise he could not pay her.[128] She could not do so, and he then said it was of no consequence. He would proceed on though the woman pressed him to take breakfast and pay her some other time. He declined and, crossing the Creek where the water would not have taken him to his knees, he is found drowned. However, by what means remains unknown. The money he had in his pocket, about five pounds, gone. The blankets he had strapped to his saddle also gone. The horse and dray [were] found by the Creekside by a shepherd. When

---

126 After being arrested on Lockyer's complaint, Jonathan Harris was incarcerated in the Goulburn Gaol on 7 July 1837 and then conveyed to Sydney and locked in the Hyde Park Barracks (where he had earlier spent his first night on Australian soil) to await his trial: see *Ancestry – NSW Gaol Description and Entrance Books 1818-1930 for Jonathan Harris* (http://tinyurl.com/y9gnyquo) (at 5 September 2020). Jonathan was tried on 8 August 1837 in the New South Wales Supreme Court before Mr Justice Burton and a Civil Jury on a charge of stealing three bullocks from Lockyer on 1 May 1836. He was found not guilty of the charge: see the *Sydney Monitor*, Wednesday, 9 August 1837, p. 2; and the *Sydney Herald*, Thursday, 10 August 1837, p. 2.

127 See the *Lockyer Letter* (http://tinyurl.com/y7k5dqxp) (at 5 September 2020).

128 The rural locality of Bogolong is now the site of the small village of Bookham, close by the junction of the Bogolong and Jugiong Creeks: see *Wikipedia – Bookham, New South Wales* (http://tinyurl.com/y4y6ubp3) (at 5 September 2020).

looking into the Creek, [the shepherd] saw the flash of a coat floating and, drawing it out, found the body of Mr Stroud, as afterwards identified, and up to this time the matter remains wrapped in mystery."[129]

Taken in context, Lockyer's account of the events surrounding the death of John Stroud is clearly structured so as to carry the implication that Stroud was murdered by Jonathan Harris. Whilst it may readily be conceded that Jonathan may not have wanted Stroud to give evidence in court against him, it should be borne in mind that Stroud died before Jonathan was charged with stealing the bullocks from Lockyer. There is precious little on the record to suggest that Stroud met his end by foul means, and there is not a scintilla of admissible evidence available to suggest that Jonathan played any part in Stroud's death. Over 180 years after that death, Jonathan is manifestly entitled to the presumption of innocence and the benefit of the doubt.

As mentioned above, there has been an indication, but no confirming evidence to date, that Jonathan Harris was granted his first Ticket of Leave at some time between his assignment to work for Elizabeth in August 1833 and her death on 30 March 1836.[130] Be that as it may, there is no doubt that he was issued with such a Ticket, as Lockyer indicated in the *Lockyer Letter*, soon after his acquittal on 8 August 1837 at his trial in Sydney.[131]

There are three things worth noting about Jonathan's 1837 Ticket of Leave. In the first place, although it was allowed in September 1837, the physical Ticket appears to have been issued on 19 February 1838. Secondly, the Ticket was allowed on the recommendation of a Sydney Bench of Magistrates. Presumably, Jonathan applied to the Magistrates for the Ticket in Sydney very shortly after his acquittal. Thirdly, the Ticket purported to restrict him to the Yass District. The Shelley brothers' *Bombowlee* run in the Tumut River valley was located in that District. Accordingly, it seems clear that when Jonathan applied for the Ticket of Leave, he envisaged that he would move to *Bombowlee* to work for the brothers or for William Shelley alone.

According to Edmund Lockyer, Jonathan did not immediately move to *Bombowlee* after his trial in Sydney in 1837. Rather, it would seem that he returned to the block he had hitherto occupied on William Shelley's *Grampian Hills* property and resumed his former employment with Shelley.[132]

It would also appear that Jonathan's brush with the New South Wales criminal justice system in 1837 did not deepen his respect for the law. Not only did he return to live and work in the Goulburn District in contravention of the requirement in his Ticket of Leave restricting him to the Yass District, but according to Edmund Lockyer, Jonathan took to keeping a sly grog shop. As Lockyer put it in the *Lockyer Letter*:

> "Jonathan Harris, as before stated, had returned to his old residence near my boundary fence, where he became a greater nuisance than ever, keeping a sly grog shop. My farm servants were frequently drunk, and though every precaution and means were taken to detect him, all failed until a sergeant of the 28th

---

129 See the *Lockyer Letter* (http://tinyurl.com/y7k5dqxp) (at 7 September 2020).. The *Sydney Herald* had this to say about John Stroud's death:
"We have been informed upon unquestionable authority, that about a month since, the body of a respectable young man named John Stroud, about twenty years of age, and an overseer to Major Lockyer, was found in Jugyong Creek, near Yass, and was afterwards buried without an inquest being held. It is not known who are the unfortunate deceased young man's connexions, but from his deportment while in the service of Major Lockyer, it is conjectured they are highly respectable. It would have been somewhat more satisfactory if it had been known by what means the young man met his death. We should like to know what the authorities are about in that direction, to allow such a circumstance to pass over unnoticed."
See the *Sydney Herald*, Thursday, 20 October 1836, p. 2. It would not be much of a leap of logic to conclude that the *Sydney Herald*'s informant of "unquestionable authority" here was in fact Edmund Lockyer

130 See footnote 125 and the accompanying text above.

131 See Ancestry – *1837 Ticket of Leave for Jonathan Harris* (http://tinyurl.com/y9gnyquo) (at 7 September 2020). See also the *Lockyer Letter* (http://tinyurl.com/y7k5dqxp) (at 7 September 2010).

132 See the *Lockyer Letter* (http://tinyurl.com/y7k5dqxp) (at 7 September 2020).

[Regiment] stationed at Towrang Stockade went in disguise as a traveller going up the country and was instantly supplied by Harris with spirits.133 The sergeant laid an information at Wingello before R. Campbell Esquire, brother-in-law of Mr Shelley. As soon as it was known, Harris immediately disappeared by removing to Mr. W. Shelley or Mr. G. Shelley's station at the Tumut River, where he remained and kept out of the way for 12 months, though a Ticket of Leave holder and ought to have mustered, which I find he did not, nor was reported."[134]

On 22 June 1839, Jonathan Harris' second child and eldest daughter, Elizabeth Harris Jnr, married William Clark in an Anglican ceremony conducted at the small settlement of Bowring around 14 km to the north-west of Goulburn.[135] The groom was 29 years of age. His bride was all of 15 years old.

William Clark had arrived in New South Wales from Kent, England as a free settler with his parents and at least one brother in about 1833. After a short time living at Sutton Forest, the Clark family moved south-west in late 1833 or early 1834 to the Yass Plains west of Goulburn where, like the other male members of his family, William almost certainly worked on a grazing property.[136]

It is not known how Elizabeth Harris met William Clark. Working for William Shelley on both the latter's *Grampian Hills* property and on *Bombowlee* in the Tumut River valley, Jonathan Harris probably became acquainted with William Clark and the other members of the Clark family as he travelled through the Yass region. Indeed, Jonathan and William Clark may have had something in common which drew them and their respective families together. Like Jonathan, William and his older brother, John Clark, were suspected by local authorities of "sly grog selling".[137]

Following their marriage, William took Elizabeth south across the Murray River to a squatting run he had earlier taken up in 1838 on the left bank of the Ovens River just downstream of its junction with the King River.

Elizabeth's marriage and move to the Ovens River probably made Jonathan Harris' life substantially more difficult. He would certainly have been deprived of her help in caring for the three younger Harris children. At the time of their sister's marriage, Sophia was 7 years old, Thomas was 5 years old and George Jarvis only 3 years of age. How Jonathan coped with his duties as a sole parent is not now known. However, what is known is that he was not a sole parent for long.

On 22 October 1840, Jonathan married his second wife, Ann Grubb, in the newly-constructed Anglican Church of St Saviour in Goulburn. At the time of this marriage, Jonathan was said to be 39 years of age and Ann 29 years old.[138]

Ann Grubb was born shortly before 29 August 1819 in or about Upway in Dorset, England. She was the

---

133 The *Towrang Stockade* was located near to the Wollondilly River and about 10 km to the east-north-east of Goulburn. It was built in about 1838 to house convicts engaged in local roadworks and, in particular, on the construction of the Great Southern Road. The convicts were guarded by soldiers from a number of British Regiments; the first contingent being with the 28th Regiment: see *Wikipedia – Towrang Convict Stockade* (http://tinyurl.com/y545dwyk) (at 7 September 2020); and *NSW Government: Towrang Convict Stockade, Associated Sites and Road Formations* (http://tinyurl.com/yyxecaoj) (at 7 September 2020).

134 See the *Lockyer Letter* (http://tinyurl.com/y7k5dqxp) (at 7 September 2020).

135 See *Register of Births, Deaths and Marriages, New South Wales – Marriages* (Vol.23B, No. 420).

136 See the *Wangaratta Chronicle*, Monday, 4 January 1993, p. 21.

137 See the *Lockyer Letter* (http://tinyurl.com/y7k5dqxp) (at 9 September 2020); the *Sydney Monitor*, Wednesday, 7 June 1837, p. 2; the *Sydney Herald*, Thursday, 8 June 1837, p. 2; and H G Martindale, *New Crossing Place: The Story of Seymour and its Shire* (1982), p. 15.

138 See *Family Search – Australian Marriages, 1810-1980: Jonathan Harris* (http://tinyurl.com/yxc6vwkb) (at 9 September 2020). As a convict Ticket of Leave holder, Jonathan Harris needed the permission of the Colonial Government to marry. He applied for that permission on or about 22 September 1840 and it was duly granted on 29 September 1840: see *Ancestry – New South Wales, Australia, Registers of Convicts, Applications to Marry, 1826-1851* (http://tinyurl.com/y9gnyquo) (at 9 September 2020); and *Ancestry – Marriage Banns, St Saviour's Church, Goulburn 1840* (http://tinyurl.com/y9gnyquo) (at 9 September 2020).

daughter of an Upway labourer, William Grubb, and his wife, Elizabeth Grubb (née Reid). Ann was baptised on 29 August 1819 in St Laurence's Church, Upway.[139] On 20 April 1840, she left Plymouth as a bounty emigrant on board the *Lady Clark* bound for New South Wales, where it was intended that she work as a housemaid. The *Lady Clark* arrived in Sydney on Friday, 14 August 1840.[140]

Ann Grubb was accompanied on her voyage to Sydney by her brother, Thomas Grubb, and the latter's wife, Sarah Grubb (née Whittle). All three moved quickly from Sydney and settled at Murrays Flat, a rural locality on the Wollondilly River approximately 7 km to the north-east of Goulburn and close to William Shelley's *Grampian Hills* property.[141]

After their marriage, Jonathan and Ann, together with the five of his children then still living with him, apparently occupied the same block on William Shelley's *Grampian Hills* property as Jonathan had earlier occupied with his first wife, Elizabeth, and their children. This kept Ann in close proximity to her kin at Murrays Flat. On 12 September 1841, Ann Harris gave birth to a son, William Thomas Harris. William was christened in St Saviour's Church, Goulburn on 3 October 1841.[142]

On 14 September 1841, just two days after William Harris' birth, Jonathan Harris was granted a replacement Ticket of Leave for his 1837 Ticket. Where the latter had restricted Jonathan to the Yass District, the new Ticket allowed him to remain in the Goulburn District.[143] The 1841 Ticket proved to have a short life-span. On 10 October 1841, the New South Wales Colonial Government granted Jonathan a Conditional Pardon. This Pardon was conditional in that it required him to remain in the Colony for the balance of his original sentence: that is, for life.[144]

It seems likely that at some point in time prior to the end of 1841, Jonathan negotiated a lease from William Shelley of all of the latter's *Grampian Hills* property. This engendered the ire of Edmund Lockyer, who wrote in the *Lockyer Letter*:

> "In December 1841 last year, to my surprise, I found he had again returned to the Grampian Hills and had actually become the tenant of Mr W Shelley's late residence when he [Shelley] having removed to Goulburn. I took an opportunity of remonstrating with Mr W Shelley upon the impropriety of letting his place to such a tenant, as he well knew the annoyance this man had been to me. He merely replied he would let it to those who would pay him and had security given him for the lease."[145]

---

139 See *Ancestry: Jonathan Harris Family Tree – Ann Grubb* (http://tinyurl.com/y2laeaj4) (at 10 September 2020); and *Ancestry – Dorset, England, Births and Baptisms, 1813-1906: Record for Ann Grubb* (http://tinyurl.com/y4fjku6z) (at 10 September 2020). In 1819, Upway was a small village around 6.5 km to the north of the town of Weymouth. It is now a suburb of Weymouth.

140 See the *Sydney Herald – Supplement Extraordinary*, Saturday, 15 August 1840, p. 1. See also *Ancestry – Unmarried Female Immigrant Certificate for Ann Grubb* (http://tinyurl.com/y6hxxtry) (at 10 September 2020). The 1840 voyage of the *Lady Clark* was promoted and arranged by the well-known London emigration agent, John Marshall: *Ibid*. See also *Australian Packet Ships: Emigration to New South Wales* (http://tinyurl.com/yyrkltew) (at 10 September 2020); and Elizabeth Rushen, *John Marshall: Ship Owner, Lloyd's Reformer and Emigration Agent* (2020), passim.

141 See Anon., "Biography of Ann Grubb" in *Ancestry: Jonathan Harris Family Tree – Ann Grubb* (http://tinyurl.com/y43n5evw) (at 10 September 2020); and Edith Medway, "Letter to the Editor" in the *Crookwell Gazette*, Monday, 5 September 2016 (http://tinyurl.com/y2ufxv9p) (at 10 September 2020).

142 See *Ancestry: Jonathan Harris Family Tree – William Thomas Harris* (http://tinyurl.com/y53d9gzg) (at 10 September 2020); and *Ancestry – Australia, Births and Baptisms, 1792-1981 for William Thomas Harris* (http://tinyurl.com/yx8p5waw) (at 10 September 2020).

143 See *Ancestry – 1841 Ticket of Leave for Jonathan Harris* (http://tinyurl.com/y9gnyquo) (at 10 September 2020).

144 See *Ancestry – 1841 Conditional Pardon for Jonathan Harris* (http://tinyurl.com/ycb4kvf4) (at 10 September 2020). Jonathan was required to pay a fee for his Conditional Pardon before it took effect and before the document evidencing it was provided to him. It seems that he may never have paid the fee and hence collected the document. An advertisement published in the *Australasian Chronicle* in Sydney on 6 December 1842 listed Jonathan as one of a number of persons invited to pay the necessary fee and collect the document: see the *Australasian Chronicle*, Tuesday, 6 December 1842, p. 4. However, by the time the advertisement was published, Jonathan was again languishing in prison.

145 See the *Lockyer Letter* (http://tinyurl.com/y7k5dqxp) (at 10 September 2020).

Jonathan Harris' married life with his second wife, Ann Harris, proved to be short. On or about 17 August 1842, Jonathan was charged at Parramatta with robbery in company with three others: his eldest son, Jonathan Harris Jnr; Cormack Berry and William Whitehouse. Details surrounding the charge are now sketchy. The following report, dated 18 August 1842, was published on 23 August 1842 in the *Australasian Chronicle*:

> "Yesterday, four men were committed to take their trial for robbing one Alfred King, and old man, at Chillick's public house, on the Sydney road, of £47. The prisoners and prosecutor had come down the country from near Goulburn in company. Two of the prisoners have been sent to Hyde Park barracks to be identified; the other two, Jonathan Harris and his son Jonathan, are committed. The father holds a Ticket of Leave. Six one pound notes, part of the property, were found concealed in one of the drays."[146]

In the *Lockyer Letter*, Edmund Lockyer provided a few further particulars relating to the offence. He wrote:

> "In September past, Harris and his son, about 21 years of age, came down to Parramatta accompanied by two bullock drivers and two teams and an old man nearly 70 years of age – a shepherd who had been in Mr Shelley's employ who held a [money] order on Messrs Tingcombe and Watkins for £47, which Harris and son, with the other parties robbed the old man of the notes after he had cashed the order."[147]

It would seem that it was Jonathan Harris Snr himself who took the £47 from Alfred King by picking that latter's pocket at Chillick's public house after King had cashed his money order.[148] Neither of the above accounts ventures to say why the men were travelling from Parramatta to Sydney together with two drays. Were they taking produce from the *Grampian Hills* property or elsewhere for sale? Were they intending to collect supplies? Were the men with Jonathan Harris Snr his employees or in the employ of another or others? Why did King have a money order from Messrs Tingcombe and Watkins, and why and where did he cash it?

Contrary to Edmund Lockyer's version of events, the robbery took place in August, and not in September, 1842. And contrary to the *Australasian Chronicle*'s report, the two Harrises were not committed for trial on 17 August 1842. As mentioned above, all four of the accused were charged with robbery on or about that date.

In point of fact, the Colonial Government's records show that the four charged men were committed on 30 August 1842 by Police Magistrate Gilbert Eliott at Parramatta to stand trial for the robbery of King at the Parramatta Quarter Sessions sittings commencing in September 1842. The trial proceeded on 10 September 1842. The two Harrises were duly convicted. For their parts, Berry and Whitehouse were acquitted. Both Harrises were sentenced to be transported to Van Diemen's Land: Jonathan Harris Snr for 15 years and his son for 10 years.[149] Jonathan Harris Jnr's sentence was subsequently commuted to transportation for seven years.[150]

Following their convictions, both of the Harrises were conveyed to Sydney, where they were lodged in the

---

146 See the *Australasian Chronicle*, Tuesday, 23 August 1842, p. 2. £47 in 1842 would be worth around $104,380 in 2021: see Measuring Worth (https://tinyurl.com/yc676z3u) (at 10 August

147 See the *Lockyer Letter* (http://tinyurl.com/y7k5dqxp) (at 11 September 2020)

148 See *Jonathan Harris' Tasmanian Convict Record* (http://tinyurl.com/y8vjyu9u) (at 13 September 2020)..

149 See *Ancestry – Parramatta Quarter Sessions Trial Register for 1842* (http://tinyurl.com/y835fbnv) (at 11 September 2020). Notwithstanding their acquittals, it seems that Berry ended up after the trial with his Ticket of Leave cancelled. Whitehouse was sent to Hyde Park Barracks as a supposed "runaway" convict from Van Diemen's Land: *Ibid*.

150 See *Ancestry: Archives Office of Tasmania – Convict Papers for Jonathan Harris Jnr* (CON37-1-1, p. 130) (http://tinyurl.com/y578j5j9) (at 12 September 2020).

Darlinghurst Gaol on 13 September 1842.[151] Jonathan Harris Jnr was held in Darlinghurst Gaol until 13 October 1842. He was then placed on board the convict ship *Waterlily* anchored in Sydney Harbour with 26 other convicts. The *Waterlily* left Sydney on 17 October 1842 bound for Van Diemen's Land. The vessel arrived at Hobart on 29 October 1842.[152] Jonathan disembarked the following day.[153]

Jonathan Harris Snr's immediate fate was a little different from that of his son. On 14 September 1842, the older Harris was transferred from Darlinghurst Gaol to Cockatoo Island Gaol in Sydney Harbour.[154] He was to remain there for just over a year. On 14 October 1843, Jonathan was taken on board the ship *Sir John Byng*, where he joined 51 other convicts destined for Van Diemen's Land. The *Sir John Byng* reached Hobart on 28 October 1843. The convicts on board were offloaded from the ship on 29 October 1843.[155]

It was noted above that Jonathan Harris' arrest, trial and incarceration in England in 1825 must have had a devastating impact on his first wife, Elizabeth Harris, and their two young children, Jonathan Harris Jnr and Elizabeth Harris Jnr. Not only were they deprived of Jonathan's support, but his enforced absence occurred at a time when Elizabeth was pregnant with their third child, Henry Harris.

History sometimes comes close to repeating itself. Jonathan's arrest, trial and incarceration in Australia in 1842 would have had an equally devastating impact on his second wife, Ann Harris, and such of Jonathan's children who were living with her on the *Grampian Hills* property leased by Jonathan from William Shelley. These children were the four youngest of the six born to Elizabeth Harris (Henry, Sophia, Thomas and George Jarvis Harris), together with Ann Harris' only child at that point, William Thomas Harris. And Ann, like Elizabeth before her, was pregnant again when Jonathan was arrested.

In late December 1842, Ann Harris was confronted with the seizure by the New South Wales Colonial Government of her imprisoned husband's property, together with the property of Jonathan Harris Jnr, and with the advice that it was the Government's intention to sell that property. Both Harris men had been convicted and gaoled for a felony. The common law doctrine of attainder, then a part of the law of New South Wales, provided that the property, both real and personal, of a convicted felon was to be forfeited to the Crown as of right.[156]

On 30 December 1842, George Stewart, the Police Magistrate at Goulburn, drafted the following Notice and forwarded it on for publication in the New South Wales Government Gazette:

> "NOTICE. — A Sale, in behalf of the Crown, of the undermentioned cattle, drays, farm produce, and household furniture, late the property of Jonathan Harris, sen. and jun., convicted of Felony, will take place at Goulburn, at noon of Saturday, the 28th day of January, 1843, viz:-
>
> 21 working bullocks, 3 steers, 2 heifers, 4 calves, 1 bull, 1 yearling bull, 1 light bay mare, branded J – I, 3 bullock drays, yokes, bows, and bullock harnesses, a paddock of wheat (about 20 acres), and sundry small articles of household furniture.

---

151   See *Ancestry – New South Wales, Gaol Description and Entrance Books, 1818-1930* (http://tinyurl.com/y9gnyquo) (at 13 September 2020). See also photo 12 below.
152   *Ibid*. See also *Rootsweb – Tasmanian Convict Ships List: "W" Ships* (http://tinyurl.com/y4fpf7kz) (at 13 September 2020).
153   See *Ancestry – Convict Arrivals in Hobart, 1842* (CON16.1.2), p. 11 (http://tinyurl.com/y37f9muz) (at 13 September 2020).
154   See *Ancestry – New South Wales, Gaol Description and Entrance Books, 1818-1930* (http://tinyurl.com/y9gnyquo) (at 13 September 2020). See also photo 13 below.
155   See *Jonathan Harris' Tasmanian Convict Record* (http://tinyurl.com/y8vjyu9u) (at 13 September 2020); and *Rootsweb – Tasmanian Convict Ship List: "S" Ships* (http://tinyurl.com/y495xvvo) (at 13 September 2020).
156   See "Legal Incidents of Imprisonment, Legal Capacity" in *Halsbury's Laws of Australia* (Lexus Nexus), at [335-320].

Persons indebted to, or having claims upon, the estate are requested to pay over to, or prove their claims before me, at the Police Office, Goulburn, on or before the day of sale."

The Notice was duly published in the Government Gazette on 10 January 1843.[157] If nothing else, the list of assets in the Notice showed that Jonathan Harris had been prospering on the *Grampian Hills* property prior to his arrest.

In response to the seizure and proposed sale of Jonathan's property, Ann Harris forwarded a Memorial to the New South Wales Governor, Sir George Gipps, via the Colonial Secretary. Also dated 30 December 1842, the Memorial materially stated:

"That your Memorialist's husband was convicted of felony at the last Sessions at Parramatta & that the whole of his property has been seized by the Crown.

That she has a family of five children without any means of supporting them.

Your Memorialist most humbly prays that you will be pleased to allow that any surplus money after debts are discharged be paid to her."[158]

It seems clear that Ann Harris was assisted in drafting and dispatching her Memorial to the Governor by William Shelley. Indeed, Shelley saw fit to endorse the Memorial with the following:

"I beg leave most respectfully to recommend [the] Memorialist to your Excellency's most merciful consideration."[159]

Notwithstanding Shelley's respectful recommendation, Sir George Gipps rejected Ann's plea. The Governor noted on her Memorial on 4 January 1843: "I regret I cannot interfere in this case".[160]

There is little doubt that Jonathan Harris' property was disposed of on 28 January 1843 or soon thereafter. It may be that William Shelley provided Ann and the Harris children with further support after Ann's Memorial was rejected by the Governor. However, it seems much more likely that they moved in with, and secured support from, Ann's brother, Thomas Grubb, and the latter's wife, Sarah Grubb, at the Grubbs' Murrays Flat residence.

---

157   See the *New South Wales Government Gazette* (No 4), Tuesday, 10 January 1843, p. 54.
158   See *Ancestry – Harris, Jonathan and Grubb, Annie, 1819-1861: Petition for Monies from Sale of Goods* (http://tinyurl.com/y7zby999) (at 14 September 2020).
159   *Ibid*.
160   *Ibid*. It seems almost certain that foreknowledge of Ann Harris' proposed Memorial, and of William Shelley's likely endorsement of that Memorial, motivated Edmund Lockyer to write the *Lockyer Letter* on 28 December 1843. Lockyer opened the letter with the following words:
  "I beg leave to state to you for the information of His Excellency the Governor the following narrative of Jonathan Harris the elder, a convict, as I hear a memorial has or is about to be presented in form of mitigation of his sentence of transportation of fifteen years to a penal settlement, passed on him at the Quarter Sessions held in Parramatta on the 10th of September last."
  Lockyer concluded his letter thus:
  "It having come to my knowledge that a petition or memorial was or is to be presented to His Excellency the Governor on behalf of these persons [Jonathan Harris Snr and Jonathan Harris Jnr], I consider I should be deficient in my duty knowing all these circumstances if I did not make them known."
  For his part, Sir George Gipps noted on the letter:
  "This will be taken into consideration if any Petition be received from Jonathan Harris or on his behalf. Take care that it is so."
  See the *Lockyer Letter* (http://tinyurl.com/y7k5dqxp) (at 14 September 2020). Lockyer may have got the gist of Ann Harris' Memorial wrong, but he seems to have at last had his revenge on Jonathan Harris.

On 6 April 1843, Ann Harris gave birth in Goulburn to her second child; a son she named George Robert Grubb Harris. The infant was christened in St Saviour's Church, Goulburn on a date in April 1843 which is now uncertain.[161] Equally, if not more, uncertain is why Ann chose to give him the first name that she did. Presumably, as at the date of the baptism, Jonathan Harris' sixth child by Elizabeth Harris, George Jarvis Harris, was still living with her. He would then have been only 7 years old.

An indent for the convicts arriving in Sydney in 1826 on board the *Marquis of Hastings* recorded that Jonathan Harris was then 5′ 6" in height, of fair complexion, blue eyed and with brown hair.[162] Upon his arrival in Hobart some 17 years later on the *Sir John Byng* in 1843, his height, complexion and eye colouring were, as one might expect, recorded in identical terms to those used in the 1826 Sydney indent. However, by 1843, his previously brown hair had turned grey, although his eyebrows and whiskers apparently remained brown. The 1843 Hobart description of Jonathan also noted that his head was round, his whiskers thin, his visage long, his forehead of medium height, his nose long, his mouth of medium width and his chin small and dimpled. He had a scar on his right arm and his left little finger was said to be "split". It was further noted that he could neither read nor write.[163]

Jonathan's life and movements in Van Diemen's Land are not easy to chart in any detail. Some of the Colonial Government's records are cryptic at best.[164] Further research delving into those records could well be productive. However, it would appear that soon after his arrival on the Island, Jonathan was taken to the Port Arthur Convict Settlement on the Tasman Peninsula around 100 km to the south-east of Hobart.[165]

The Port Arthur Convict Settlement has been described as:

"the destination for those deemed the most hardened of British criminals, those who were secondary offenders, having re-offended after their arrival in Australia."[166]

The daily work of the convicts ranged from labour in gangs, including timber getting, vegetable gardening and cereal growing and harvesting, to relatively skilled labour in shipyards and artificers' shops. Over time, agriculture and timber getting increased in importance. Many of the convicts were required to work wearing leg irons. Convicts were all at significant risk of being punished for infractions of the rules by whippings or sensory deprivation in solitary confinement.[167]

How Jonathan Harris fared during his time at Port Arthur is currently unknown. However, given his age

---

161 See *Ancestry: Jonathan Harris Family Tree – George Robert Grubb Harris* (http://tinyurl.com/y4eol8y8) (at 15 September 2020). An anonymous biography of George asserts that:

"His NSW Baptism Certificate states he was born on the 6 April 1843 to parents, Jonathan Harris, Farmer and wife, Ann Harris from Goulburn. The date of baptism states 1 April 1843, which appears to be transcribed incorrectly. The Baptism was at the Church of England, St. Saviour and the Minister was William Sowerby, who also married his parents in 1840. George Robert was also baptised on the 5 November 1848 at the Church of England, Gunning, the same day as Elizabeth Ann Olliver and church records note his parents as William & Ann Olliver. His birth is stated on this record as 5 January 1843. This second Baptism has led to confusion by some that Ann had two sons by the name of George."

See Anon., "George Robert Grubb Harriss" in *Ancestry: Foster-Wood Family Tree – George Robert Grubb Harriss* (http://tinyurl.com/y5g9fnhj) (at 15 September 2020).

162 See footnote 91 and the accompanying text above.

163 See *Jonathan Harris' Tasmanian Convict Record* (http://tinyurl.com/y8vjyu9u) (at 20 September 2020).

164 See, in particular, *Jonathan Harris' Tasmanian Convict Record* (http://tinyurl.com/y8vjyu9u) (at 20 September 2020).

165 Ibid. See also Cooper, *Biography of Jonathan Harris* (http://tinyurl.com/ycuhrduv) (at 20 September 2020); and photo 14 below.

166 See *Wikipedia – Port Arthur, Tasmania* (http://tinyurl.com/y5twbqp8) (at 20 September 2020).

167 See Richard Tuffin, "Port Arthur Penal Settlement" in *Companion to Tasmanian History* (http://tinyurl.com/y2b6gpdv) (at 20 September 2020).

and rural background, there is a fair chance that he was engaged for at least part of that time in cultivating fruit and vegetables for the Settlement.[168]

In all, Jonathan probably spent less than two years imprisoned at Port Arthur before being transferred to the Bridgewater Convict Station "on probation" for three months.[169] This Probation Station was located at Granton on the right bank of the Derwent River some 19 km to the north-west of Hobart. Convicts sent to it were required to work in chain gangs maintaining the main road between Hobart and Launceston (which crossed the Derwent River from Granton to Bridgewater on the opposite bank by a convict-constructed causeway and bridge); together with building and repairing local roads. The convicts laboured to quarry and crush nearby rock deposits for road fill, and worked with picks and shovels on the roads themselves. It was clearly hard and demanding work. [170]

The Van Diemen's Land Probation System, which was unique to the Island, was introduced in 1839 and, in various guises, lasted until 1853 and the abolition of transportation. Michael Sprod has outlined the System in the following manner:

> "All convicts were to be subjected to successive stages of punishment, commencing with a period of confinement and labour in gangs: at a penal settlement for life-sentenced prisoners, or at a probation station for all others. If they progressed satisfactorily through several stages of decreasing severity, they received a probation pass and became available for hire to the settlers. Gangs of passholders awaiting employment remained at the station and continued to labour on public works."[171]

Following his three month period of probation at the Bridgewater Convict Station, Jonathan Harris was "classed" (assessed) by the Colonial authorities with respect to his future.[172] There is no reason to think that this assessment led to any extension of his period of probation. In all likelihood, he would have received his probation pass; making him available for hire by settlers.

Settler employment of probation passholders in Van Diemen's Land after 1840 was regulated by convict labour contracts. Under these contracts:

> "the working relationship was governed by a fixed-term contract negotiated between the colonial government, private employer and convict passholder. Any of the three parties could terminate the contract, under specific guidelines (e.g. employers had to give 10 days' notice or 10 days' pay; passholders could appeal to the Comptroller-General to leave). Convicts could refuse any or all offers of employment. Wages

---

168   By 1840, about 16 hectares of land around Port Arthur were being farmed for vegetables; with mainly potatoes and cabbages being cultivated. Wheat was also being widely grown. In August of that year, some 3,000 bushels of wheat grown at the Settlement were transported for sale in Hobart: see David Cameron, *Convict-Era Port Arthur: Misery of the Deepest Die* (2021), p. 175; and the *Colonial Times*, Tuesday, 25 August 1840, p. 7. It is of interest to note that on the Marriage Certificate which accompanied Jonathan's third marriage (to Mary Ann Squire) in Hobart on 20 June 1853, his "rank" (or occupation) was said to be that of a gardener: see Ancestry – *Jonathan Harris and Mary Ann Squire: Marriage Certificate, 1853* (http://tinyurl.com/y7t8qp3u) (at 20 September 2020).

169   See *Jonathan Harris' Tasmanian Convict Record* (http://tinyurl.com/y8vjyu9u) (at 20 September 2020). Jonathan must have been transferred to the Bridgewater Convict Station in or before 1845. In that year, the Convict Station ceased to function as a Probation Station. Thereafter, it functioned simply as a road construction and repair convict station until its closure in about 1849: see Geoff Ritchie, "Bridgewater Convict Station" in *On The Convict Trail* (http://tinyurl.com/y2plszkm) (at 20 September 2020).

170   Ibid. See also photo 15 below.

171   See Michael Sprod, "Probation System" in *Companion to Tasmanian History* (http://tinyurl.com/y56ty6oy) (at 20 September 2020). See also Cameron, *op. cit.*, pp. 80 and 194.

172   See *Jonathan Harris' Tasmanian Convict Record* (http://tinyurl.com/y8vjyu9u) (at 20 September 2020). See also Cooper, *Biography of Jonathan Harris* (http://tinyurl.com/ycuhrduv) (at 20 September 2020).

were to be paid to convicts, both monetary and in kind. In the original system of 1840, contracts ran for a minimum of one month to a maximum of one year; wages were fixed at £9 per annum for a male convict, and £7 per annum for a female convict; rations and clothing were specified; and health cover provided."[173]

It is not presently known when Jonathan first secured a convict labour contract with a free settler in Van Diemen's Land, or how many such settlers he worked for in all. What is known is that by January 1848, he was working for a man currently known only as "Willet".[174] On 31 January 1848, Jonathan was sentenced to two months hard labour in chains for "insolence" to Willet.[175] Where he served this sentence is not presently known. Nor is his fate immediately after serving it known. However, it seems almost certain that he continued to work under the convict labour contract system as a hired worker; perhaps even in the ongoing employment of Willet.

There can be no doubt that Jonathan Harris would have wished to truncate his period of controlled servitude if possible and as quickly as possible. It seems that in late 1848, he applied to the Van Diemen's Land Colonial Government for a Ticket of Leave. Perhaps not surprisingly given his punishment for "insolence" earlier in that year, his application was refused on 3 November 1848. However, it appears that Jonathan was advised by the authorities to apply again in three months' time.[176] He did apply again after about three months and, on 13 February 1849, he was duly granted a Ticket of Leave.[177]

Jonathan was recommended for a Conditional Pardon on 26 February 1850.[178] However, for a reason or reasons not currently known, it would seem that a Conditional Pardon was not immediately forthcoming.

On 1 October 1850, Jonathan's Ticket of Leave was revoked.[179] The reason for its revocation is not presently known. One can only assume that it involved some probably minor infraction of the web of rules which continued to govern his life a convict. Notwithstanding this backward step, Jonathan's life was to change within a month. On 26 October 1850, he was hired to work for his older half-brother, George Allcorn.[180]

It will be recalled that after being convicted in Lewes, Sussex of receiving stolen goods on 10 December 1831, George Allcorn had been sentenced to be transported to the colonies for seven years. He sailed from Plymouth on the *York* for Van Diemen's Land on 11 August 1832 and arrived in Hobart on 29 December 1832.[181]

George Allcorn did not remain in Hobart for long following his arrival. In early 1833, he was assigned to work for Ronald Gunn, who had been appointed in 1830 as the Superintendent of Convicts for the Northern Division

---

173   See *Digital Panopticon: VDL Convict Labour Contracts, 1848-1857* (http://tinyurl.com/y5vkl8a9) (at 20 September 2020).

174   See *Jonathan Harris' Tasmanian Convict Record* (http://tinyurl.com/y8vjyu9u) (at 20 September 2020).

175   *Ibid*. It is conceivable that the "Willet" for whom Jonathan Harris was working in January 1848 was William Willett, the Master of the Van Diemen's Land Government vessel, the *Lady Franklin*: see *The Courier* (Hobart), Wednesday, 14 June 1848, p. 2. The *Lady Franklin* was a 269 ton barque built at Port Arthur and launched in late December 1841. A good deal of its service life was spent ferrying convicts between Hobart, Port Arthur and Norfolk Island: see Cameron, *op. cit.*, pp. 201-202. William Willett was seemingly a disciplinarian; the sort of person who might well have been very sensitive to actual or perceived insolent words directed at him: see the *Sydney Morning Herald*, Thursday, 21 June 1855, p. 3. However, this is pure conjecture. There are very likely to have been other settler Willets (or Willetts) in Van Diemen's Land at about this time.

176   See *Jonathan Harris' Tasmanian Convict Record* (http://tinyurl.com/y8vjyu9u) (at 21 September 2020). See also Cooper, *Biography of Jonathan Harris* (http://tinyurl.com/ycuhrduv) (at 21 September 2020); and John M J Fitzpatrick, "The Adventurous Life of Jonathan Harris (1800-1891) of Benalla", (June 2017) 33(6) *Ancestor* 16, at 18.

177   See *Jonathan Harris' Tasmanian Convict Record* (http://tinyurl.com/y8vjyu9u) (at 21 September 2020). Notice of the grant of the Ticket of Leave was published in the *Cornwell Chronicle* (Launceston) on 17 February 1849: see the *Cornwell Chronicle*, Saturday, 17 February 1849, p. 384.

178   See *Jonathan Harris' Tasmanian Convict Record* (http://tinyurl.com/y8vjyu9u) (at 21 September 2020).

179   *Ibid*. See also Fitzpatrick, *op. cit.*, p. 18.

180   See *Ancestry – Register of Convicts Hired by Private Employer, 1850-1852* (http://tinyurl.com/ybrpe6cy) (at 21 September 2020); and *Jonathan Harris' Tasmanian Convict Record* (http://tinyurl.com/y8vjyu9u) (at 21 September 2020).

181   See footnotes 80 and 82, together with their accompanying texts, above.

of Van Diemen's Land based in Launceston.[182] Whilst in Gunn's service, George probably worked as a ploughman and performed other agricultural labouring duties.

George Allcorn worked for about a year assigned to Ronald Gunn. Then, on 12 April 1834, he was convicted of stealing vegetables and fruit from Gunn's garden and sentenced to 12 months' hard labour in a chain gang. He very likely served this sentence at the Bridgewater Convict Station, which some 10 or 11 years later housed his younger half-brother, Jonathan Harris.

Prior to his conviction and transportation, George had married Frances Relph in St Thomas-à-Becket's Church, Brightling, Sussex.[183] They had at least three children together in England. Maria Allcorn was born in 1826; Edward Allcorn in 1829; and George Allcorn Jnr either in late 1831 or early 1832.[184]

Whilst George Allcorn was still completing his sentence for stealing Ronald Gunn's vegetables and fruit, Frances Allchorn and her three children took ship on board the *Janet* to sail to Hobart to join her husband and their father. Leaving England on 22 July 1834, they arrived in Hobart on 2 December 1834.[185] With her husband imprisoned at the time of her arrival in Hobart, Frances Allcorn naturally found life extremely difficult in a foreign land. For a time, she was forced to surrender the care of her two older children to the King's Orphan School in Hobart.[186]

Following the completion of his sentence, George Allcorn was assigned in early 1835 to work as an agricultural labourer for a George Peevor in the Richmond district of Van Diemen's Land.[187] Frances Allcorn, together with George Allcorn Jnr, likely joined George on Peevor's property soon afterwards. On 1 July 1835, the couple were able to retrieve their daughter, Maria Allcorn, from the King's Orphan School. Edward Allcorn was similarly delivered by the School to their care on 6 October 1836.[188]

George and Frances Allcorn had three further children together in Van Diemen's Land. Louisa Allcorn was born in 1836. Unfortunately, she died of influenza in 1839. Frances Hannah Allcorn was born in 1839, and Ann Jane Allcorn was born in 1840.[189]

It is not clear when George Allcorn was granted his Ticket of Leave. However, it does seem certain that he secured his Certificate of Freedom, which left him free of all residual convict restraints, on or shortly after 10 December 1838.[190]

Maree Alcorn, a descendant of George and Frances Allcorn, has provided some useful information on her ancestors' later years in Hobart in an online periodical, *Westhobart*. On 9 July 2014, she wrote:

"In 1841 and 1843, the censuses show George and family living west of Hobart as tenants in a stone

---

182   See *Ancestry: 1833 Convict Assignment List – George Allchorne* (http://tinyurl.com/yd3902b2) (at 21 September 2020).
183   See *Family Search – Frances Relph (1799-1884)* (http://tinyurl.com/y8346hl5) (at 21 September 2020); and *My Heritage – George Allcorn* (http://tinyurl.com/ydacp4t3) (at 21 September 2020).
184   See *Family Search – Frances Relph (1799-1884)* (http://tinyurl.com/y8346hl5) (at 21 September 2020).
185   See the *Hobart Town Courier*, Friday, 5 December 1834, p. 3.
186   See *Friends of the Orphan Schools: Orphan No. 29 – Edward Alcorn* (http://tinyurl.com/y889knhb) (at 21 September 2020); and *Convict Records – George Allcorn* (http://tinyurl.com/yd55e59d) (at 21 September 2020).
187   See *Ancestry: 1835 Tasmania List of Convicts – George Allchorne* (http://tinyurl.com/ydcmfwv3) (at 21 September 2020).
188   See *Friends of the Orphan Schools: Orphan No. 29 – Edward Alcorn* (http://tinyurl.com/y889knhb) (at 21 September 2020); and *Convict Records – George Allcorn* (http://tinyurl.com/yd55e59d) (at 211 September 2020).
189   See *Family Search – Frances Relph (1799-1884)* (http://tinyurl.com/y8346hl5) (at 22 September 2020); *Convict Records – George Allcorn* (http://tinyurl.com/yd55e59d) (at 22 September 2020); and *Friends of the Orphan Schools: Orphan No. 29 – Edward Alcorn* (http://tinyurl.com/y889knhb) (at 22 September 2020).
190   See the *Hobart Town Courier*, Friday, 30 November 1838, p. 2; and *Ancestry – George Allcorn's Convict Release* (http://tinyurl.com/ybah6xe6) (at 22 September 2020).

cottage called "the Pigeon House" on Knocklofty, owned by S. Ross (Susannah, née Smith, widow of James Ross, a.k.a. Dr. James Ross). George was working as a gardener for Susannah Ross and is believed to have grown grapes at this time.

James Ross was a schoolmaster who was tutor to Governor Arthur's children in 1825. He became a prominent and influential publisher.... In 1832, he was granted 312 acres (126 ha), Paraclete, on Knocklofty, making him one of the earliest settlers in the Mount Stuart area. He built a homestead in the vicinity of Summerhill Road (now West Hobart) and a substantial stone pigeon house on Knocklofty. It is believed that he had ambitions to lay out botanical gardens but it never came to fruition....

"Pigeon Houses" were so called because on their 2nd storey, high-pitched roof line and possibly some people kept pigeons in the roof. The Pigeon House was demolished many years ago.... Knocklofty is above Cascade Road/Upper Macquarie Street, where they [the Allcorns] subsequently lived....

On 28 June 1848, George Allcorn acquired two pieces of land, one in Macquarie Street and one in Washington Street in the Electoral District of Queensborough, now known as South Hobart."[191]

George and Frances Allcorn moved with their children from Knocklofty to a property on nearby Cascades Road, Cascades at some presently unknown point in time prior to George engaging Jonathan Harris to work for him. George very likely cultivated his property on the flank of Mount Wellington as a market garden. Precisely how, where and when the two half-brothers caught up with each other in Van Diemen's Land are matters now lost in time. Jonathan's convict labour contract with George of 26 October 1850 obliged the former to work for the latter at George's Cascades property for six months and for a total wage of £9.0.0.[192]

On 5 November 1850, Jonathan was given a 5/- reward by the Van Diemen's Land Colonial Government.[193] The reason for this gift is not known. Presumably, it was for some act on Jonathan's part which was perceived to benefit the Government. Accordingly, it may be of no coincidence that Jonathan's Ticket of Leave was restored to him shortly afterwards on 17 December 1850.[194]

Although Jonathan's convict labour contract with George Allcorn was expressed to be of six months' duration, there can be little doubt that Jonathan continued working for George for some considerable time after the contract had formally expired. With his Ticket of Leave restored, he would have done so without overt Government supervision. On 25 March, 1851, he lodged an application for a Conditional Pardon.[195] This was granted to him on 15 April 1851. The Conditional Pardon gave Jonathan freedom of movement, save that he was restrained from returning to the United Kingdom or entering Ireland.[196]

---

191 See *Westhobart – Knocklofty* (Maree Alcorn, 9 July 2014) (http://tinyurl.com/y7m5qeyl) (at 22 September 2020). See also Caroline Evans and Kathryn Evans, *Understanding the Contemporary Cultural Values of Knocklofty Reserve*, p. 9; and *Friends of the Orphan Schools: Orphan No. 29 – Edward Alcorn* (http://tinyurl.com/y889knhb) (at 22 September 2020).

192 See *Ancestry – Register of Convicts Hired by Private Employer, 1850-1852* (http://tinyurl.com/ybrpe6cy) (at 22 September 2020). It is of interest to note that in the *Register* entry, the name of Jonathan's employer was originally written as "George Allcorn". The word "Allcorn" was then crossed out and replaced with "Halcorn". Presumably, the alteration was made by the author of the entry. In all probability, the latter had asked George his name, written it down correctly and then had doubts about what he had heard. Enquiring again, he likely misinterpreted George's articulation of his surname to be "Halcorn", rather than "Allcorn". Such a misinterpretation could well have been due to George speaking with a broad Sussex accent: see *Wikipedia – Sussex Dialect* (http://tinyurl.com/y2s6hcdn) (at 22 September 2020). The fact that George was illiterate and made his mark against the *Register* entry rather than signed it would not have helped.

193 See *Jonathan Harris' Tasmanian Convict Record* (http://tinyurl.com/y8vjyu9u) (at 22 September 2020).

194 *Ibid*. See also *The Hobart Town Gazette*, Tuesday, 17 December 1850; and Fitzpatrick, *op. cit.*, p. 18.

195 See *Jonathan Harris' Tasmanian Convict Record* (http://tinyurl.com/y8vjyu9u) (at 22 September 2020).

196 See *Ancestry – Jonathan Harris' Conditional Pardon, Hobart Town, 1851* (http://tinyurl.com/y9gnyquo) (at 22 September 2020). Although the Conditional Pardon was dated 15 April 1851, it was not formally registered by the Colonial Government until 17 May 1851: see *Ancestry – Tasmania, Convict Court and Selected Records 1800-1899 for Jonathan Harris* (http://tinyurl.com/yay2zmdv) (at 22 September 2020).

It was very probably while Jonathan Harris was still working for George Allcorn that Jonathan first met his future third wife, Mary Ann Squire.

Mary Ann Squire was probably born in about 1828 to Philip and Ann Squire.[197] She is on record as asserting that she was born in the town of Great Torrington in Devon, England.[198] Her father almost certainly worked as an agricultural labourer. He apparently died in 1838 when Mary Ann was about 10 years of age.[199] Life would undoubtedly have been hard for her during her childhood and adolescence. She almost certainly had no formal education and could neither read nor write.[200]

According to the 1851 *England Census*, Mary Ann Squire described herself as a "glover" by trade.[201] It is at least possible that she had been apprenticed at an early age to a glove maker in Great Torrington.

It appears that Mary Ann Squire had not reached adulthood when she first ran foul of the law. At the Devon Quarter Sessions which commenced in Plymouth on 20 October 1845, it seems that she was convicted of larceny and sentenced to be imprisoned for four months.[202] She was around 18 years of age at the time of her trial. Four years later, when Mary Ann was about 22 years old, she was again gaoled for larceny after stealing "wood". During the Devon Quarter Sessions in Devonport, which commenced on 16 October 1849, she was sentenced to three weeks gaol – a surprisingly light sentence in view of her earlier conviction at Plymouth.[203]

Mary Ann Squire's run of larceny convictions in England culminated in her conviction for that offence at the Devon Quarter Sessions which commenced in Exeter on 2 July 1850. Mary Ann was charged with having stolen a purse containing silver with a value of 9/- from a Jane Dowling in Great Torrington on 25 May 1850.[204] Upon her conviction on 30 July 1850 of the offence, and with the Court noting that she had previously been convicted of felony, she was sentenced to be transported "beyond the seas" for seven years.[205]

Following her sentencing, Mary Ann attempted to hang herself in her cell in Exeter Castle, using her bonnet ribbon. She was cut done before she died by a Constable Cole and found to have suffered a "considerable injury", from which she fully recovered in due course.[206]

On 31 August 1850, Mary Ann was taken from Exeter Castle to the Millbank Prison at Westminster to await

---

197   See W. McCrea, *Surgeon's Journal of the Anna Maria Convict Ship* (http://tinyurl.com/y53s09r8) (at 26 September 2020); and *Ancestry – Marriage Record of Jonathan Harris to Mary Ann Squire in Hobart Town* (http://tinyurl.com/y4f79w8t) (at 26 September 2020). Mary Ann's parents names are recorded on her Death Certificate: see *Ancestry – Mary Ann Harris in Australia: Death Index, 1787-1985* (http://tinyurl.com/y7h8pfmm) (at 26 September 2020).

198   According to an unnamed genealogical archivist at the Devon Record Office, Mary Ann Squire gave her age in the 1851 *England Census* as 23 and her place of birth as Torrington, Devon. She also stated that she was a "glover" by trade. At the time of this census, she was a prisoner in the Millbank Prison at Westminster awaiting transportation to Australia: see *Ancestry – Devon Research re Mary Ann Squire* (http://tinyurl.com/yxgceakw) (at 26 September 2020). There is apparently no record of a Mary Ann having been christened in Great Torrington at any relevant time. However, the Parish Records of the Church of St Mary and St Gregory in the small village of Frithelstock some 4.5 km to the west of Great Torrington contains an entry for the marriage of Philip Squire and Mary Hore on 10 April 1813. Nine children born to Philip and Mary Squire were christened in Frithelstock's St Mary and St Gregory's Church between 1813 and 1832. However, Mary Ann Squire is not listed as one of them. Philip Squire was recorded as being a labourer by occupation, and it may be that his work took him and his family temporarily to Great Torrington in or about 1828, where Mary Ann was born. She may not have ever been christened. Alternatively, she might have been baptised in an as yet unascertained neighbouring parish where Philip Squire later worked: *Ibid*. It might be noted that Philip and Mary Squire's youngest child, Charlotte Squire, was apparently living with or near to Mary Ann I Great Torrington in 1850: *Ibid*; and see Cooper, *Biography of Mary Ann Squire – Convict* (http://tinyurl.com/y3krcxse) (at 26 September 2020).

199   See *Ancestry: Jonathan Harris Family Tree – Mary Ann Squire* (http://tinyurl.com/yx8q8tmb) (at 26 September 2020).

200   Mary Ann "made her mark", rather than signed, her Marriage Certificate upon her marriage to Jonathan Harris on 20 June 1853: see *Ancestry – Marriage Record of Jonathan Harris to Mary Ann Squire in Hobart Town* (http://tinyurl.com/y4f79w8t) (at 26 September 2020).

201   See footnote 198 above.

202   See *Ancestry – England and Wales, Criminal Registers, 1791-1892 for Mary Ann Squire, 1845* (http://tinyurl.com/y43utgca) (at 26 September 2020)

203   See *Ancestry – England and Wales, Criminal Registers, 1791-1892 for Mary Ann Squire, 1849* (http://tinyurl.com/y35uk7lz) (at 26 September 2020).

204   See Cooper, *Biography of Mary Ann Squire – Convict* (http://tinyurl.com/y3krcxse) (at 26 September 2020).

205   See *Ancestry – England and Wales, Criminal Registers, 1791-1892 for Mary Ann Squire, 1850* (http://tinyurl.com/yyfawkwq) (at 26 September 2020).

206   See Cooper, *Biography of Mary Ann Squire – Convict* (http://tinyurl.com/y3krcxse) (at 26 September 2020).

her transportation.[207] After languishing in Millbank Prison for over a year, she was placed on board the *Anna Maria* convict ship at Woolwich; one of 200 female convicts and 46 children from workhouses. The *Anna Maria*, a barque of 421 tons built in 1836, sailed from Woolwich bound for Van Diemen's Land on 6 October 1851.[208]

The voyage of the *Anna Maria* from England to Van Diemen's Land was apparently an unpleasant one; marked by storms, foul winds, cold weather and boisterous seas. Many of the convict women suffered attacks of dysentery. Mary Ann Squire suffered two such episodes, which were evidently successfully treated with turpentine, castor oil and laudanum. By the end of the voyage, four of the women and six of the children had died. The *Anna Maria* arrived at Hobart on 26 January 1852, and its reluctant passengers disembarked soon afterwards.[209]

After her arrival in Tasmania, Mary Ann Squire was described in her Convict Record as being 5′ 3″ high; with a fair complexion, a round head, brown hair and eyebrows, an oval visage, a medium forehead, hazel eyes, and with a mouth, nose and chin all also described as medium. She was recorded as being a country servant, rather than a glover.[210]

After leaving the *Anna Maria*, Mary Ann was probably taken to the Cascades Female Factory to the immediate south of Hobart. This facility was located in close proximity to both Knocklofty and Cascades Road, and was the primary site in Hobart for the reception and incarceration of women convicts.[211] The Cascades Female Factory served as a hiring depot, holding convicts awaiting hire into the service of settlers.[212] In addition to being held at the Cascades Female Factory, Mary Ann probably spent some time during 1852 at the Brickfields Hiring Depot at New Town.[213]

Over the course of 1852 and early 1853, it would seem that Mary Ann was hired out as a domestic servant to a Mr Warham of Brisbane Street, Hobart; to Richard Chilton of the *High Plains* property near Deloraine; and to Edmond Hodgson of Macquarie Street, Hobart. Her service with Chilton could not have been a happy time for Mary Ann. On 9 August 1852, she was ordered to serve four days in a cell for disobedience of his orders.[214]

It is not now known how or when Jonathan Harris initially met Mary Ann Squire. Their first meeting may have occurred while Mary Ann was living at the Cascades Female Factory and Jonathan was working for George Allcorn on the latter's Cascades Road property nearby. Alternatively, they may have met whilst both were attending to business matters in Hobart for the men they worked for respectively.

In any event, Jonathan and Mary Ann applied to the Van Diemen's Land Colonial Government on or about 18 May 1853 for permission to marry. Their application was approved a week or so later on 25 May 1853.[215] They were married on 20 June 1853 in St George's Anglican Church, Battery Point. Jonathan's half-brother and sister-in-law, George and Frances Allcorn, were the official witnesses to the marriage.[216] It was no doubt a happy occasion for

---

207   See *Ancestry – Millbank Prison Register Entry for Mary Ann Squire* (HO 24/12) (http://tinyurl.com/y2fegu7k) (at 26 September 2020).
208   See *Convict Records – Anna Maria Convict Ship* (http://tinyurl.com/yycfx4jl) (at 26 September 2020); and McCrea, *Surgeon's Journal of the Anna Maria Convict Ship* (http://tinyurl.com/y53so9r8) (at 26 September 2020).
209   Ibid. See also Cooper, *Biography of Mary Ann Squire – Convict* (http://tinyurl.com/y3krcxse) (at 26 September 2020).
210   See Tasmanian State Archives, *Convict Conduct Record for Mary Ann Squire* (CON41/1/32 Image 165) (http://tinyurl.com/y29x99te) (at 26 September 2020). ("Mary Ann Squire's Tasmanian Convict Record").
211   See Australian Government, *National Heritage Places – Cascades Female Factory* (http://tinyurl.com/y2hmsvco) (at 27 September 2020).
212   See Female Convicts Research Centre, *Hiring Depots* (http://tinyurl.com/yxkj7krb) (at 27 September 2020).
213   Ibid. See also *Mary Ann Squire's Tasmanian Convict Record* (http://tinyurl.com/y29x99te) (at 27 September 2020).
214   Ibid. See also Cooper, *Biography of Mary Ann Squire – Convict* (http://tinyurl.com/y3krcxse) (at 27 October 2020).
215   See *Ancestry – Jonathan Harris and Mary Ann Squire: Permission to Marry, 1853* (http://tinyurl.com/y9gnyquo) (at 28 September 2020).
216   See *Ancestry – Marriage Record of Jonathan Harris to Mary Ann Squire in Hobart Town* (http://tinyurl.com/y4f79w8t) (at 28 September 2020). See also photo 16 below.

both Jonathan and Mary Ann. The only fly in the ointment was the fact that Jonathan was still married to his second wife, Ann Harris.

As mentioned above, Jonathan's arrest, trial and incarceration in 1842 left Ann Harris living on the *Grampian Hills* property leased by Jonathan from William Shelley, and with the care of Jonathan's four youngest children by his first wife, Elizabeth Harris (Henry, Sophia, Thomas and George Jarvis Harris), together with her own son, William Thomas Harris. Ann was also left pregnant with her second child by Jonathan. The confiscation and sale of all of Jonathan's property by the New South Wales Colonial Government in February 1843 would have left Ann destitute.[217] It seems likely that Ann and the children moved in with, and secured support from, Ann's brother and his wife, Thomas and Sarah Grubb at the Grubbs' Murrays Flat residence.

On 6 April 1843, Ann Harris gave birth in Goulburn to her second child ; a son she named George Robert Grubb Harris. The infant was subsequently baptised in St Saviour's Church, Goulburn later in that month.[218]

If Ann did move in with her brother and sister-in-law following Jonathan Harris' arrest, trial and incarceration, it would seem that she did not live with them for long. Perhaps as early as in 1843, she began cohabiting with William Olliver. The latter was born at Portsea in Hampshire, England and worked for the most part as a baker and confectioner. Between 1848 and 1858, Ann had four children by William Olliver. These were:

- Elizabeth Olliver; born shortly before 5 September 1848 in Gunning, New South Wales;
- Henry Olliver; born shortly before 11 March 1851 in Gunning;
- Rebecca Olliver; born shortly before 17 July 1856 in Goulburn; and
- Jane Olliver; born shortly before 3 July 1858 in Goulburn.[219]

On 18 February 1861, Ann Harris married William Olliver in the Wesleyan Parsonage in Goulburn. On the Marriage Certificate, Ann described herself as a widow, and William described himself as a widower. Ann's brother and sister-in-law, Thomas and Sarah Grubb, were the official witnesses to the marriage.[220] Just 10 months later, Ann died of heart disease on 30 December 1861 at Burrangong near Young in New South Wales.[221] She was 42 years old when she died and was buried in the Young Cemetery.[222]

The marriages of Jonathan Harris to Mary Ann Squire and of Ann Harris to William Olliver were void in law but very likely not bigamous. In *Walker v Walker*, Mr Justice Barber observed in the Supreme Court of Victoria:

> "In England, bigamy was punished canonically, but was not an offence punishable by the civil courts until 1603. In that year, the Statute of James I (I Jac. c. 2) made bigamy a felony, but the Act excepted persons whose husband or wife 'should have remained seven years beyond the sea, or the same period within his Majesty's dominions and not known by the other to be living': see Bishop on Divorce, 1852 ed., p. 161. The exception, changed in verbiage but not in substance, has remained in the statutes ever since....

---

217 See footnote 160 and the accompanying text above.

218 See footnote 161 and the accompanying text above.

219 See *Ancestry: Jonathan Harris Family Tree – Ann Grubb* (http://tinyurl.com/y2laeaj4) (at 28 September 2020); and *Ancestry: Jonathan Harris Family Tree – William Olliver* (http://tinyurl.com/y3foto45) (at 28 September 2020). It has been asserted that George Robert Grubb Harris, Ann's second son by Jonathan Harris, was re-baptised under the name George Robert Olliver in company with the baptism of his half-sister, Elizabeth Olliver in Goulburn on 5 September 1848: see Anon., "Biography of Ann Grubb" in *Ancestry: Jonathan Harris Family Tree – Ann Grubb* (http://tinyurl.com/y43n5evw) (at 28 September 2020).

220 See *Ancestry – William Olliver and Ann Harriss, Marriage Certificate 1861* (http://tinyurl.com/y6bepoxx) (at 28 September 2020).

221 See *Ancestry – Ann Olliver (née Grubb), Death Certificate 1861* (http://tinyurl.com/y5xeywl7) (at 28 September 2020); and *Ancestry: Jonathan Harris Family Tree – Ann Grubb* (http://tinyurl.com/y2laeaj4) (at 28 September 2020).

222 See *Ancestry – Ann Olliver (née Grubb): Grave in Young Cemetery* (http://tinyurl.com/y5qvy5x4) (at 28 September 2020); and Anon., "Biography of Ann Grubb" in *Ancestry: Jonathan Harris Family Tree – Ann Grubb* (http://tinyurl.com/y43n5evw) (at 28 September 2020). William Olliver died at Forbes on 4 January 1886: see *Ancestry: Jonathan Harris Family Tree – William Olliver* (http://tinyurl.com/y3foto45) (at 28 September 2020).

> The effect in any particular case of the spouse not having been heard of for seven years and not known to be alive during that period would appear to be to save the contracting party from a prosecution for bigamy, but not to validate the marriage. For example, on the re-appearance of the missing spouse, the marriage would not be valid."[223]

Jonathan had been separated from Ann for over 10 years when he married Mary Ann Squires. Ann had been separated from Jonathan for over 18 years when she married William Olliver. Almost certainly, all contact between Jonathan and Ann ceased after Jonathan was removed from New South Wales to Van Diemen's Land in 1843. Although both may well have had their suspicions, neither would likely have known the other to be still living during or after seven years of forced separation.

The newly married Mary Ann Harris was granted a Ticket of Leave by the Van Diemen's Land Colonial Government on 4 October 1853.[224]

On 26 April 1854, Mary Ann gave birth to her first child; a son whom she and Jonathan named Edward Harris.[225] It is of interest to note that the *Jonathan Harris Family Tree* website claims that Jonathan and Mary Ann Harris had another son in Tasmania in "about 1854": George Harris.[226] However, the website provides no authority for its inclusion of this George Harris amongst Jonathan and Mary Ann's children. Nor would it seem that a George Harris, born in Van Diemen's land in about 1854, is mentioned elsewhere. If, in fact, he ever existed, he could have been a twin of Edward Harris who was either stillborn or died very soon after birth.

On 19 December 1854, Mary Ann Harris was granted a Conditional Pardon.[227]

A little short of a year after Edward Harris' birth, on 4 April 1855, Mary Ann gave birth to Walter Harris.[228] Jonathan and Mary Ann were living in Harrington Street, Hobart when both Edward and Walter Harris were born.[229] Jonathan's occupation after his marriage to Mary Ann and their move to live in the Harrington Street premises is unknown. He may have continued to work for George Allcorn. Alternatively, he may have found work closer to his new home.

The Conditional Pardons granted to Jonathan and Mary Ann ostensibly left them free to move with their children from Van Diemen's Land to the Australian mainland if and when they chose. They made their choice to do so at some point in time between Walter Harris' birth in Van Diemen's Land in 1855 and the birth of their next authenticated child, Francis Harris, in Victoria in late 1857; with the move most likely occurring during 1856 or early 1857.[230]

---

223   [1969] VR 580, at p. 584. See also Henry Finlay, *To Have But Not To Hold: A History of Attitudes to Marriage and Divorce in Australia 1855-1975* (2005), pp. 29-30.

224   See *Mary Ann Squire's Tasmanian Convict Record* (http://tinyurl.com/y29x99te) (at 1 October 2020); and Cooper, *Biography of Mary Ann Squire – Convict* (http://tinyurl.com/y3krcxse) (at 1 October 2020).

225   See *Ancestry: Jonathan Harris Family Tree – Edward Harris* (http://tinyurl.com/y6jdwpub) (at 7 October 2020)

226   See *Ancestry: Jonathan Harris Family Tree – George Harris* (http://tinyurl.com/y2rvdp42) (at 7 October 2020).

227   See *Mary Ann Squire's Tasmanian Convict Record* (http://tinyurl.com/y29x99te) (at 7 October 2020)

228   See *Births in the District of Hobart, 1855 – Walter Harris* (http://tinyurl.com/yc5coo7k) (7 October 2020); Cooper, *Biography of Mary Ann Squire – Convict* (http://tinyurl.com/y3krcxse) (at 7 October 2020); and *Ancestry: Jonathan Harris Family Tree – Walter Harris* (http://tinyurl.com/y2tp32qh) (at 7 October 2020).

229   See Cooper, *Biography of Mary Ann Squire – Convict* (http://tinyurl.com/y3krcxse) (at 7 October 2020); and *Births in the District of Hobart, 1855 – Walter Harris* (http://tinyurl.com/yc5coo7k) (at 7 October 2020).

230   Edward Harris' obituary in 1934 stated that he had arrived in Benalla from Tasmania at the age of two years: see the *North Eastern Ensign*, Friday, 16 March 1934, p. 3. If correct, this would place his family's move from Tasmania in 1856. However, a death notice published in the *Sydney Morning Herald* after Jonathan's death on 4 October 1891 observed that he had been a resident of Benalla for 34 years: see the *Sydney Morning Herald*, Tuesday, 6 October 1891, p. 5. See also the *Euroa Advertiser*, Friday, 9 October 1891, p. 3. This would put the Harris family's arrival in Benalla in 1857.

It might be noted that the name of the southern island colony was changed from Van Diemen's Land to Tasmania on 1 January 1856: see Terry Norman, "Tasmania, The Name" in *The Companion to Tasmanian History* (http://tinyurl.com/yc4ob2g3) (at 2 October 2020).

Following his return to the mainland, Jonathan Harris probably had no further contact with his half-brother, George Allcorn. The latter died in West

Although their Conditional Pardons left Jonathan and Mary Ann Harris ostensibly free to move from Tasmania to the Australian mainland, Victorian law at the time of their move arguably did not permit them entry into Victoria. The *Convicts Prevention Act 1854* (Vic), enacted on 16 November 1854, provided for the arrest and trial of any person who had at any time been found guilty of any capital or transportable felony in Britain, Ireland or any British possession other than Victoria, and had at any time after the passing of the Act come into Victoria. A person convicted of breaching the Act could, at the discretion of the Court, be given seven days to return to the place he or she had come from, or be taken in custody to that place, or be sentenced to be imprisoned, with or without hard labour, for up to three years and then forced to leave Victoria. The Act further stated that all property belonging to offenders was to be seized and, at the discretion of the Court, forfeited to the Crown and sold.[231]

The *Convicts Prevention Act 1854* contained an important saving provision. Section 1 of the Act provided that:

> "[N]othing in this Act contained shall apply or be deemed to apply to any person whose sentence, or sentences if more than one, shall have expired for a greater period than three years previous to his arrival in Victoria."

On the assumption that they first arrived in Victoria during 1856 or early 1857, the question arises as to whether Jonathan and Mary Ann would have been entitled to the benefit of this proviso.

Jonathan received his Conditional Pardon on 15 April 1851. At that point in time, his September 1842 New South Wales sentence of transportation for 15 years still had 6½ years to run. However, his original 1825 Sussex sentence was one of transportation for life. Could it be said that Jonathan's Conditional Pardon resulted in the expiration of both sentences within the meaning of the *Convicts Prevention Act 1854*? The Conditional Pardon left him a free man save in the he was unable to return to Britain or enter Ireland. Did that limiting qualification prevent his 1842 sentence from expiring until September 1857 and the completion of the 15 year term? Did it also prevent his original 1825 sentence from ever expiring? The point is moot. Accordingly, it is at least possible that Jonathan, for one, made his entry into Victoria in breach of the *Convicts Prevention Act 1854*; rendering him potentially liable to its penalties.

Hobart on 26 January 1867: see *Deaths in the District of Hobart, 1867 – George Allcorn* (http://tinyurl.com/yd965hjr) (at 7 October 2020); and *The Mercury*, Monday, 28 January 1867, p. 1. George Allcorn's wife, Frances Allcorn, died in Hobart on 11 July 1884: see *Westhobart – Knocklofty (Maree Alcorn, 9 July 2014)* (http://tinyurl.com/y7m5qeyl) (at 7 October 2020); and *The Mercury*, Saturday, 12 July 1884, p. 1.

231 See *An Act to Prevent the influx of Criminals into Victoria* (18 Vict. No. 3). Soon after white settlers arrived in what was then the Port Phillip District of New South Wales, escaped convicts, Ticket of Leave holders and others granted Conditional Pardons began crossing Bass Strait from Van Diemen's land. The discovery of gold in what became the Colony of Victoria in 1851 dramatically increased their number; to the consternation of free settlers in the new Colony. In the words of Edward Sweetman:

"When news of the rich goldfields in Victoria reached Van Diemen's Land in 1851, these people came over in greatly increased numbers. The city of Melbourne and other parts of the Colony became inundated with convicts from Van Diemen's Land. Deeds of violence committed by them were common; the colonists became seriously alarmed. The question of preventing further ingress of convicts into Victoria from Van Diemen's Land was regarded as crucial at the elections for the Legislative Council. Candidates' addresses published in the newspapers almost invariably stated that those seeking election regarded the convict question as one demanding immediate attention. The firm stand taken later by the elected members of the Legislative Council upon the convict question was due largely to the fact that they represented public opinion on the matter."

See Edward Sweetman, *Constitutional Development in Victoria, 1851-5* (1920), pp. 148-9 (http://tinyurl.com/y4ga4ukk) (at 7 October 2020). An earlier version of the 1854 Act was enacted by the Victorian Colonial Legislation in 1852: see *An Act to Facilitate the Apprehension and Prevent the Introduction into the Colony of Victoria of Offenders Illegally at Large* (16 Vict. No. 13). This earlier Act was disallowed by the Imperial Government in London; with the Secretary of State for the Colonies, the Duke of Newcastle, advising Lieutenant Governor La Trobe by dispatch dated 30 April 1853 that his Government regarded the act as "a practical interference with the Queen's prerogative of pardon": see Sweetman, *op. cit.*, p. 151. Whilst the Imperial Government at no time expressly approved of the subsequent 1854 Act, it did not disallow the measure: see Sweetman, *op. cit.*, p. 159. The 1854 Act was later continued in its operation by further Victorian Acts: see 19 Vict. No. 3; 21 Vict. No 16; and 22 Vict. No 68. It was finally repealed in 1900: see s. 2 of, and the First Schedule to, the *Crimes Act 1900* (Vic) (54 Vict. No. 1079). See also Patrick Morgan, "The Vandemonian Trail: Convicts and Bushrangers in Eastern Victoria" in (1998) 74 Island 52.

For her part, Mary Ann had been sentenced in Sussex in July 1850 to transportation for seven years. This sentence would have therefore expired in July 1857; leaving her eligible to lawfully enter Victoria in July 1860. However, Mary Ann was granted her Conditional Pardon on 19 December 1854. Even if this Conditional Pardon can be construed for the purposes of the *Convicts Prevention Act 1854* as having resulted in the expiration of her sentence, the earliest she could have lawfully entered Victoria would have been in December 1857. It therefore seems likely that Mary Ann, and quite possibly Jonathan, entered Victoria illegally.[232]

Margaret Cooper has suggested that after Jonathan's arrival in Victoria:

> "It is likely that Jonathan snr. and jnr. had travelled to the Victorian goldfields and discovered gold which funded the purchase of their properties. The 1853 'Bendigo Goldfields Petition' contains the name Jonathan Harris. Jonathan Harris Jnr's death notice has an unusual mention of him being the first finder of gold in Hustler's Reef, Sandhurst."[233]

However, given that Edward Harris was born in Hobart in 1854, it seems highly unlikely that Jonathan Harris Snr, as distinct from his eldest son Jonathan Harris Jnr, signed the Bendigo Goldfields Petition in 1853. Indeed, it seems that there is no evidence available to suggest that Jonathan Harris Snr ventured to the Bendigo or any other goldfield upon his arrival in Victoria. If Edward Harris was only two years old when he arrived in Benalla from Tasmania (as was asserted in Edward's 1934 obituary[234]), then it seems likely that Jonathan, Mary Ann and their two young sons settled almost immediately in Benalla after their move to Victoria and without any Bendigo deviation.

It is not entirely clear why Jonathan Harris chose to settle in Benalla with Mary Ann and their two young children. It is likely that the fact that his eldest daughter, Elizabeth Clark (née Harris), was living with her husband, William Clark, and their growing family at Wangaratta some 38 km to the north-east of Benalla played a significant part in the decision.[235] Moreover, it appears that Jonathan's sixth child, George Jarvis Harris, was probably living in either Wangaratta or Benalla at about the time that Jonathan moved to Benalla.[236] It may have

---

232 Janet McCalman has observed that:

"It was meant to be 'Victoria the Free', uncontaminated by the Convict Stain. Yet they came in their tens of thousands as soon as they were cut free or able to bolt. More than half of all those transported to Van Diemen's Land as convicts would one day settle or spend time in Victoria. There they were demonised as Vandemonians. Some could never go straight; a few were the luckiest of gold diggers; a handful founded families with distinguished descendants. Most slipped into obscurity."

See McCalman, *op. cit.*, front endpaper. She has further observed that:

"...perhaps 30,000 possible expirees and absconders crossed [from Van Diemen's Land] into Victoria. And looking at the criminal records, perhaps under 2,000 men were to offend again, and over 200 of the women."

See McCalman, *op. cit.*, p. 111.

233 See Cooper, *Biography of Mary Ann Squire – Convict* (http://tinyurl.com/y3krcxse) (at 7 October 2020). See also *Eurekapedia – The Bendigo Goldfields Petition* (http://tinyurl.com/yxw7bwuo) (at 7 October 2020); and Dorothy Wickham, "The 1853 Bendigo Goldfields Petition" in *Ballarat Heritage Services* (http://tinyurl.com/yym7ef58) (at 7 October 2020).

234 See footnote 230 above.

235 It might be added that at the time of Jonathan's arrival in Benalla, Elizabeth Clark's brother-in-law, Richard Clark, was the owner of the *Black Swan Inn* in the village: see Alan J. Dunlop, *Benalla Cavalcade: A History of Benalla and District* (1973), p. 36; and the *Benalla Ensign and Farmer's and Squatter's Journal*, Saturday, 13 January 1872, p. 2. At the time of his death in 1869, Richard Clark owned at least 63 properties in and around Benalla: see the *Ovens and Murray Advertiser*, Tuesday, 9 February 1869, p. 4.

236 George Jarvis Harris' first wife, Annie Harris (née Brown), gave birth to the couple's first child, Georgina Harris, in Wangaratta at some stage in 1857: see *Ancestry: Jonathan Harris Family Tree – Georgina Annie Harris* (http://tinyurl.com/y3rr8b9j) (at 7 October 2020). George Jarvis and Annie may have been living in Wangaratta at the time of the birth. However, it is possible that they were living in Benalla; with Annie travelling to Wangaratta to secure the assistance of her sister-in-law, Elizabeth Clark, with the birth of Annie's first child. George Jarvis and Annie Harris' second child, Elizabeth Harris, was born in Benalla in 1859: see *Ancestry: Jonathan Harris Family Tree – Elizabeth Sophia Harris* (http://tinyurl.com/y6e5vyvg) (at 7 October 2020). See also Jenny Coates, "Jonathan Harris and his Australian progeny" in *Conversations with Grandma* (http://tinyurl.com/ycxmzlg7) (at 7 October 2020).

been that Jonathan was able to lease or otherwise occupy good, rich riverine land to farm close to the Broken River at Benalla, and that that was pivotal to his decision to settle there. Similar land close to the Ovens or King Rivers at or near to Wangaratta could well have been already taken and unavailable to him.

After his arrival in Benalla, it is likely that Jonathan commenced growing vegetables for sale. In 1858, it seems that he was able to purchase land in order to pursue his farming business on Market Street, near to the left bank of the Broken River and to the south of the then-course of the Sydney to Melbourne road. This land was purchased not in Jonathan's own name but in that of his four year old son, Edward Harris.[237]

Why Jonathan purchased his first block of land in Benalla in his young son's name is not clear. However, he could well have done so in an attempt to save the property from Crown seizure and sale in the event that Jonathan was arrested and convicted under the provisions of the *Convicts Prevention Act 1854*.[238] In any event, it would seem that Edward Harris subsequently raised his own family and lived out his days on the land in question.[239]

On 24 April 1860, Jonathan Harris bought two adjoining allotments of land in his own name on Garden Street; just to the east of the Market Street land held in Edward Harris' name. The Garden Street allotments probably extended further east to an anabranch of the Broken River.[240] Like the possibly contiguous Market Street land, Jonathan undoubtedly farmed his Garden Street properties as a market garden. He may also have raised cattle on part of the land or elsewhere nearby.[241] Jonathan and Mary Ann lived out the remainder of their respective lives in a six room brick and weatherboard house Jonathan constructed on the Garden Street land.[242]

It would seem that Jonathan and Mary Ann Harris had seven children together whilst they lived in Benalla. The first of these children, Francis Harris, was born on 20 October 1857. He died and was buried in Benalla on 27 November 1857 after living for a mere 38 days.[243] Francis died prior to the registration in Benalla of the birth of Jonathan and Mary Ann's sixth child, Frederick Harris, on 16 July 1862. The registration entry completed on that day for Frederick refers to the fact that Francis Harris, born between the births of Walter and Albert Harris, was then deceased.[244]

The six remaining children born to Jonathan and Mary Ann Harris in Benalla were:

- Albert Harris, born in about 1858;[245]
- Frances Alice Harris, born on 15 July 1860;[246]
- Frederick Harris, born on 23 May 1862;[247]
- John Phillip Harris, born on 16 June 1864;[248]

---

237 See Cooper, *Biography of Jonathan Harris* (http://tinyurl.com/y6zb2kad) (at 7 October 2020); and Cooper, *Biography of Mary Ann Squire – Convict* (http://tinyurl.com/y3krcxse) (at 7 October 2020).

238 See footnote 231 and the accompanying text above.

239 See Cooper, *Biography of Mary Ann Squire – Convict* (http://tinyurl.com/y3krcxse) (at 8 October 2020).

240 See the Benalla Map below.

241 See Cooper, *Biography of Jonathan Harris* (http://tinyurl.com/y6zb2kad) (at 8 October 2020).

242 See Cooper, *Biography of Mary Ann Squire – Convict* (http://tinyurl.com/y3krcxse) (at 8 October 2020). See also the *Inventory of Assets and Liabilities of the Estate of the late Mary Ann Harris*, 19 July 1899 (Public Records Office of Victoria ("PROV"): VPRS 28/P2 Unit 519, Item 72/109).

243 See *Burials in the Parish of Benalla, County of Moira, 1857-1858* – Francis Harris, p. 1; and Cooper, *Biography of Mary Ann Squire – Convict* (http://tinyurl.com/y3krcxse).

244 See *Ancestry: Frederick Harris Birth Registration Entry, 1862* (http://tinyurl.com/y52cfsnj) (at 8 October 2020). Jonathan Harris provided the relevant particulars for the Registration Entry as Informant. See also *WikiTree – Francis Harris (1857)* (http://tinyurl.com/y237w6ac) (at 8 October 2020).

245 See *Ancestry: Jonathan Harris Family Tree – Albert Harris* (http://tinyurl.com/y6rf3mcj) (at 8 October 2020).

246 See *Holy Trinity Anglican Church, Benalla: Baptismal Register, January 1855-December 1919* (referred to hereafter as "the *Holy Trinity Baptismal Register*"), p. 16 – Frances Alice Harris, 1860; and *Ancestry: Jonathan Harris Family Tree – Frances Alice Harris* (http://tinyurl.com/y3fvgkf4) (at 8 October 2020).

247 See the *Holy Trinity Baptismal Register*, p. 23 – Frederick Harris, 1862; *Ancestry: Jonathan Harris Family Tree – Frederick Harris* (http://tinyurl.com/y2kczue8) (at 8 October 2020); and *Ancestry: Frederick Harris Birth Registration Entry, 1862* (http://tinyurl.com/y52cfsnj) (at 8 October 2020).

248 See the *Holy Trinity Baptismal Register*, p. 30 – John Phillip Harris, 1864; *Ancestry: Jonathan Harris Family Tree – John Phillip Harris* (http://tinyurl.

- Charlotte Rebecca Harris, born on 30 May 1866;[249] and
- Lucy Rosetta Harris, born on 12 March 1872.[250]

Jonathan Harris was 71 years old when his last child, Lucy Harris, was born.

On Wednesday, 1 May 1872, Jonathan was one of the official witnesses to the marriage in Holy Trinity Church, Benalla of his grand-daughter, Alice Rebecca Clark, to William Moore.[251] Alice was the daughter of Jonathan's second oldest child, Elizabeth Clark (née Harris).

If 1872 brought joy to Jonathan and Mary Ann with the birth of Lucy Harris and the marriage of Alice Clark, 1873 brought great sadness. On Saturday, 1 February 1873, Elizabeth Sophia Harris, a daughter of George Jarvis Harris and Annie Harris, and Jonathan's grand-daughter, drowned in the Broken River. She was 14 years old when she died. Her death was reported in the *North Eastern Ensign* in the following terms:

> "A young girl named Elizabeth Sophia Harris, granddaughter of Mr. Harris, of Benalla, with whom she had been residing for some time past, was drowned in the Broken River on Saturday evening. Miss Harris, with some companions, had gone into the river to bathe, close to her grandfather's residence, when, unfortunately, she got beyond her depth, and before assistance could be rendered her, she had sunk. The body was speedily recovered, but all efforts to restore animation proved unavailing. Dangerous as are most of the Australian rivers, the Broken River is especially so, no less than three persons having been drowned in it, close to the town of Benalla, within the last month."[252]

In 1877, tragedy struck Jonathan again after his son, Albert Harris, was killed after being thrown from his horse on Wednesday, 17 January in that year.[253]

On Monday, 19 May 1879, Jonathan Harris had what appears to have been his last adverse encounter with the law. On that day, he was fined one shilling in the Benalla Police Court for neglecting to send a child to school. The identity of the child in question is not now known. It may be that being without any formal schooling and being illiterate himself, Jonathan did not hold the Victorian compulsory education system in high regard.

Later in the same year, 1879, Jonathan moved onto the offensive. No doubt using one of his children as his amanuensis, he wrote a letter to the Benalla Shire Council complaining of "a large sheet of water" at the end of Garden Street which he said made it impassable for foot travellers. Presumably, the water was the remains of flood water from the Broken River lying at the northern end of the street. In any event, at its meeting on Monday, 30 June 1879, the Council resolved to take no action in regard to the matter.[254]

Three years later, in 1882, and this time in company with two others, Jonathan again wrote to the Benalla Shire Council. In their letter, the three complained of "the impassable state of Market Street". On this

---

com/y4vot6ax) (at 8 October 2020); and *Ancestry: John Phillip Harris Birth Registration Entry, 1864* (http://tinyurl.com/yxj8ttg3) (at 8 October 2020).

249 See *Holy Trinity Baptismal Register*, p. 37 – Charlotte Rebecca Harris, 1866; and *Ancestry: Jonathan Harris Family Tree – Charlotte Rebecca Harris* (http://tinyurl.com/y2oh29wz) (at 8 October 2020).

250 See *Holy Trinity Baptismal Register*, p. 47 – Lucy Rosetta Harris, 1872; and *Ancestry: Jonathan Harris Family Tree – Lucy Rosetta Harris* (http://tinyurl.com/y5yenmkj) (at 8 October 2020).

251 See *Victorian Marriage Certificate – William Moore and Alice Rebecca Clark* (http://tinyurl.com/y2nuj9lx) (at 8 October 2020). The second official witness was Alice's sister, Jemima Maria Clark. See also Cooper, *Biography of Jonathan Harris* (http://tinyurl.com/y6zb2kad) (at 8 October 2020)

252 See the *North Eastern Ensign*, Tuesday, 4 February 1873, p. 2. See also *The Argus*, Saturday, 8 February 1873, p. 1.

253 See the *Evening News* (Sydney), Monday, 22 January 1877, p. 2.

254 See the *Ovens and Murray Advertiser*, Tuesday, 1 July 1879, p. 3. Flooding of the Broken River was no doubt a regular problem for the Harris family. On 25 October 1870, they were temporarily driven from their home by rising flood waters: see the *Benalla Ensign and Farmer's and Squatter's Journal*, Friday, 28 October 1870, p. 2; and Margaret Cooper, "Mary Ann *Squire* Harris" in *Find A Grave Memorial* (http://tinyurl.com/y2w2nhsx) (at 10 October 2020).

occasion, it would appear that the Council agreed on Friday, 1 September 1882 to undertake some remedial work on the road.[255]

On 20 July 1881, Jonathan's eldest child, Jonathan Harris Jnr, died at Axedale near Bendigo of the effects of hydatid disease of the liver. He had been suffering from the condition for some 10 years prior to his death.[256] At some point in time, and probably shortly before he died, he secured a visit from his father. It would have been a sad trip for Jonathan Harris Snr. The Administration Account completed on 17 December 1882 by Harriett Harris, Jonathan Harris Jnr's widow and executrix, following her late husband's death recorded a disbursement of £8 to: "Jonathan Harris Snr for travelling expenses and attendance, paid at the request of deceased."[257]

On 6 March 1885, the Harrises purchased six acres (approximately 2.4 hectares) of land in Egmont Street, Benalla, close to its intersection with Maud Street. The land was purchased in Mary Ann's name.[258] Why it was purchased in her, rather than Jonathan's, name is unclear. However, given the fact that Jonathan was then 84 years old, it may have been effected in that way in an exercise of estate planning to minimise probate duty on his estate. As with the other nearby Harris properties, the land was likely used for market gardening.

The last years of Jonathan Harris' life appear to have been uneventful. Possibly the best extant photograph of him shows him as an old man seated in a cane chair. He is flanked on each side by a young woman who almost certainly would have been one of his daughters. He holds an infant – almost certainly a grandchild – on his left knee. His face betrays none of the hardships he had undergone over the course of his long life.[259]

Jonathan died at his home on Garden Street, Benalla on Sunday, 4 October 1891. Although he died in the midst of an influenza epidemic, his cause of death was said in his Death Registration Entry to have been "senile decay".[260] He was around 91 years old when he died. There appears to have been no obituary published to mark his life and death. Jonathan was buried in the Benalla Cemetery on Wednesday, 7 October 1891. Interestingly, the officiating clergyman, the Reverend Alexander McConnon, was a Presbyterian rather than an Anglican.[261]

Jonathan Harris led a tumultuous life. Born into rural poverty at the bottom of the social hierarchy in Sussex, deserted by his biological father as an infant, and with a mother who was seemingly unable or unwilling to teach him respect for the law, it is hardly any wonder that he found himself in the dock at the Horsham Assizes in 1825 – on trial for his life.

Sentenced to death, it was always probable that rather than taking him to the gallows, Jonathan's sentence would be commuted to transportation for life to New South Wales. However, transportation meant that he was never again to see his mother or any other members of his family save for his half-brother, George Allcorn.

---

255 See the *North Eastern Ensign*, Tuesday, 5 September 1882, p. 2.

256 See *Deaths in the District of Axedale, 1881 – Jonathan Harris* (No 6405/1881). Hydatid disease is a condition caused by cysts commonly found in the liver and containing the larval stages of the dog tapeworm, *Echinococcus granulosis*. People usually become infected by handling dogs or consuming contaminated food or water: see Queensland Government, *Hydatid Disease* (http://tinyurl.com/y3zpl24v) (at 9 October 2020).

257 See the *Administration Account for the Estate of the late Jonathan Harris*, 17 December 1882 (PROV: VPRS 28/PO Unit 260, Item 22/473).

258 See Cooper, *Biography of Mary Ann Squire – Convict* (http://tinyurl.com/y3krcxse) (at 10 October 2020); Cooper, *Biography of Jonathan Harris* (http://tinyurl.com/y6zb2kad) (at 10 October 2020); and the *Inventory of Assets and Liabilities of the Estate of the late Mary Ann Harris*, 19 July 1899 (PROV: VPRS 28/P2 Unit 519, Item 72/109).

259 See photo 17 below.

260 See *Deaths in the District of Benalla, 1891 – Jonathan Harris* (No 13479/1891) (http://tinyurl.com/y929asjj) (at 10 October 2020). Jonathan's son, Frederick Harris, was the Informant for the purposes of Jonathan's Death Registration Entry. According to that Entry, Jonathan fathered 14 children. Conspicuously missing from the list were his two children by his second wife, Ann Harris (née Grubb); *Ibid*. It could well be that neither Mary Ann Harris nor her children were ever informed of Ann Harris' existence, or at least of the existence of Jonathan's two children by her: William Harris and George Robert Grubb Harris. See also the *Sydney Morning Herald*, Tuesday, 6 October 1891, p. 5; and the *Euroa Advertiser*, Friday, 9 October 2020).

261 See *Deaths in the District of Benalla, 1891 – Jonathan Harris* (http://tinyurl.com/y929asjj) (at 10 October 2020). See also photo 18 below.

Deprived of any formal education in England, and unable to read or write, Jonathan was nonetheless clearly a man of some intelligence. He must also have been a man of some charm; eliciting the practical support and perhaps friendship of significant local men in New South Wales such as Charles Tompson, William Shelley and Henry Antill. Reunited with his first wife, Elizabeth Harris, and his three oldest children, he appeared to be well on his way to making a success of his life in the Colony.

However, transportation to New South Wales clearly did not teach Jonathan respect for the law or other peoples' property. His continuing propensity to commit theft led to the enmity of another significant New South Wales settler, Edmund Lockyer, and ultimately to further transportation in 1843; this time to Van Diemen's land.

Life in the island Colony for Jonathan would have been harsh. It involved a spell in notorious Port Arthur and periods of hard labour on the roads in chains. It would have been almost as hard for his second wife, Ann Harris, and his children left behind in New South Wales. Arguably, one of the saddest things about Jonathan's life is that by virtue of his transportation to Van Diemen's Land, he had only the briefest contact with his seventh son, William Thomas Harris, and no contact whatsoever with his eighth son, George Robert Grubb Harris.

If life was hard for Jonathan in Van Diemen's Land, it at least led to an apparently happy and successful union with his third wife, Mary Ann Harris. His move to Victoria in about 1856 with Mary Ann and their two young sons was seemingly also a success. Fathering a further seven children with Mary Ann after their arrival in Benalla, it appears that Jonathan was able both to establish and operate a successful market garden on the outskirts of the town and to win the respect of the local townsfolk.

Life presented Jonathan Harris with a number of significant ups and downs. His apparent ability to navigate these ups and downs to a respected old age stands as a testament to his will and determination. His was a remarkable life.

It seems that Jonathan did not leave a Will. However, it also seems that at some stage prior to his death, he conveyed his Garden Street properties to Mary Ann.[262] Again, this could have been done with a view to avoiding probate duty.

Mary Ann Harris survived he late husband by almost eight years. Little of her life after Jonathan's death is known. Although she almost certainly had no formal education, she was described in the Benalla Rates Rolls as a "nurse".[263] Her nursing activities, which were likely centred around her children and grandchildren, were. no doubt of a very practical nature – and probably no less efficacious for that. Her interests and opinions must have extended beyond home and family. In 1891, the year of Jonathan's death, she allowed her name to be added to the Victorian *Women's Suffrage Petition*.[264]

Mary Ann died in Benalla on Monday, 3 July 1899 of the effects of a stroke. She was 73 years old when she died. Following a funeral service conducted at Holy Trinity Church in Benalla by the Reverend Joseph Allen, she was buried beside her late husband in the Benalla Cemetery on Wednesday, 5 July 1899.[265] On Friday, 7 July 1899, the *North Eastern Ensign* wrote this of Mary Ann's passing:

---

262 See the *Inventory of Assets and Liabilities of the Estate of the late Mary Ann Harris, 19 July 1899* (PROV: VPRS 28/P2 Unit 519, Item 72/109).

263 See Cooper, *Mary Ann Squire – Convict* (http://tinyurl.com/y3krcxse) (at 10 October 2020).

264 See Cooper, "Mary Ann *Squire* Harris" in *Find A Grave Memorial* (http://tinyurl.com/y2w2nhsx) (at 10 October 2020). This Petition, which was laid before the Victorian Parliament, called for Victorian women to be granted both the right to vote and the right to stand for Parliament. It was signed by some 30,000 women and is said to have been the largest known petition produced during the Nineteenth Century: see Kate Follington, *PROV: 1891 Women's Suffrage Petition* (http://tinyurl.com/yxqbj3b2) (at 10 October 2020).

265 See *Deaths in the District of Benalla, 1899 – Mary Ann Harris* (No 8398/1899). See also *Ancestry: Jonathan Harris Family Tree – Mary Ann Squire* (http://

"Mrs Harris, one of the oldest and most esteemed residents of Benalla West, has died during the past week, her remains being interred on [Wednesday] last. Mr W. G. Abbott conducted the mortuary arrangements, his new hearse attracting attention as the funeral cortege proceeded through the town. The Rev. J. Allen, vicar of Holy Trinity Church, performed the obsequies at the grave."[266]

Mary Ann Harris executed her Will on 22 January 1898. In it, she appointed her eldest and youngest children, Edward Harris and Lucy McLeod (née Harris), to be her Executors.[267] In turn, they secured a Grant of Probate of the Will in the Supreme Court of Victoria on 2 August 1899.[268] By the terms of the Will, Mary Ann:

- devised and bequeathed that part of her land in Garden Street, Benalla comprised in Allotment 8 and part of Allotment 7, Section 1D in the Parish of Benalla, together with her house, furniture goods and chattels situated thereon and her two cows, to Lucy McLeod;
- devised that part of her land in Garden Street comprised in Allotments 5 and 6, Section 1C to her son Frederick Harris; and
- devised her land in Egmont Street, Benalla comprised in Allotment 22, Section 4 to her son John Harris.[269]

Mary Ann left nothing in her will to her sons, Edward and Walter Harris, or to her daughters, Frances McEwan (née Harris) and Charlotte O'Brien (née Harris). Edward already had the Harris land in Market Street, Benalla in his own name.[270] However, Mary Ann's reasons for excluding Walter, Frances and Charlotte from sharing in her estate are not known.

---

tinyurl.com/y4jp2bwb) (at 11 October 2020); and photo 18 below.
266 See the *North Eastern Ensign*, Friday, 7 July 1899, p. 3.
267 See *Will of Mary Ann Harris, 1898* (PROV: VPRS 28/P2 Unit 519, Item 72/109).
268 See *Grant of Probate dated 2 August 1899* (PROV: VPRS 28/P2 Unit 519. Item 72/109).
269 See *Will of Mary Ann Harris, 1898* (PROV: VPRS 28/P2 Unit 519, Item 72/109).
270 See footnote 237 and the accompanying text above.

JONATHAN HARRIS' CHILDREN

Not the least of Jonathan Harris' accomplishments was the fact that he fathered 17 children with three wives on two different continents and in three different Australian colonies. Through these children, he now has a legion of descendants. And what became of Jonathan's 17 children? What follows is a brief outline of the life of each of them.

Jonathan Harris Jnr

As mentioned above, following his conviction on 10 September 1842 in Parramatta for robbery, Jonathan Harris Jnr was sentenced to be transported to Van Diemen's Land for 10 years. He left Sydney with 26 other convicts on the *Waterlily* on 17 October 1842 and arrived at Hobart on 29 October 1842; disembarking from the vessel on the following day.[271]

Jonathan served 2½ years under probation in Van Diemen's Land, and was then moved to a number of different locations around the Island Colony. On about 16 September 1847, his sentence was reduced from 10 to seven years; no doubt for good behaviour on his part. On 9 November 1847, he received a Ticket of Leave. Finally, on 6 June 1848, he was given a Conditional Pardon.[272]

Details of Jonathan's life after he secured his Conditional Pardon in Van Diemen's Land are sketchy. He must have departed the Island for Victoria at some stage between securing that Conditional Pardon in 1848 and marrying in Melbourne in 1852. On 2 April 1852, Jonathan married Harriet Hipwell Pearce in St Peter's Anglican Church, Melbourne.[273]

Jonathan's most notable achievement following his arrival in Victoria was his discovery in 1853 of *Hustlers Reef*: one of the richest gold reefs in Bendigo.[274] The fact of his discovery of the reef is clear. However, some of the published accounts of the discovery, and indeed of Jonathan's identity, appear to be replete with errors.

The first published account of Jonathan's discovery appears to be found in Robert Brough Smyth's *The Gold Fields and Mineral Districts of Victoria*, first published in 1869. Brough Smyth was a geologist and Secretary of the Victorian Department of Mines. In his book, he stated that he had acquired his history of the discovery

---

271 See footnotes 149, 150, 151 and 152, together with their accompanying texts, above.

272 See *Ancestry: Archives Office of Tasmania – Convict Papers for Jonathan Harris Jnr* (CON37-1-1, p. 130) (http://tinyurl.com/y578j5j9) (at 12 October 2020).

273 See *My Heritage – Jonathan Harris, 1822-1881* (http://tinyurl.com/yb4f6cks) (at 12 October 2020); *Ancestry: Jonathan Harris Family Tree – Jonathan Harris* (http://tinyurl.com/yxh6butb) (at 12 October 2020); *WikiTree – Jonathan Harris (1822-1881)* (http://tinyurl.com/y7qoep7p) (at 12 October 2020); and Cooper, *Biography of Jonathan Harris* (http://tinyurl.com/y6zb2kad) (at 12 October 2020).

274 Jonathan discovered gold on a section of the reef protruding through the surface of the ground on the northern slope of Mac's Hill, just south of Ironbark Gully: see Herbert Whitelaw, "Hustler's Line of Reef, Bendigo" in *Bulletins of the Geological Survey of Victoria*, No. 33 (1914), p. 9; and James Flett, *A Pictorial History of the Victorian Goldfields* (1970), p. 48. The discovery site is now encompassed within the *Hustlers Reef Reserve* located off Hustlers Road in Bendigo: see Walking Maps, *Hustlers Reef Gold Miners Heritage Walk* (http://tinyurl.com/y849ewmr) (at 3 March 2021).

Hustlers Reef has been described as the third most important of the Bendigo gold reefs: see Arthur Palmer, *The Gold Mines of Bendigo* (1979), Book 2, p. 83. The reef extended for some 13 km through the centre of Bendigo; crossing Pall Mall at its intersection with View Street: see Whitelaw, *op. cit.*, p. 9. Overall, the reef is credited with producing 953,200 ounces (about 27,023 kg) of gold: see Palmer, *op. cit.*, p. 83. It was one of the first of Bendigo's reefs to be worked by way of quartz mining.

In 1897, the *Bendigo Independent* described the reef as "a hill full of wealth": see the *Bendigo Independent*, Saturday, 29 May 1897, p. 2. In time, many mines were sunk along the reef. In 1873, the English novelist Anthony Trollope observed that:

"among all names at Sandhurst [the former name for Bendigo], the greatest name, the most thriving, the best known, and the name in highest repute is – 'Hustler'. Whence came the appellation I do not distinctly know, but I believe that there was once, - perhaps still is, - a happy Hustler."

See Anthony Trollope, *Australia and New Zealand* (1873), Vol. 2, p. 75. See also Frank Cusack, *Bendigo, a history* (2002), p. 122.

The *Great Extended Hustlers Mine* was developed in and after 1868 at the location where Jonathan first found gold on the reef. The shaft of this mine ultimately reached a depth of around 1,058 metres: see Whitelaw, *op. cit.*, p. 9.

from Jonathan Latham and John Watson; who were subsequent owners of the claim on *Hustlers Reef* originally purchased by Jonathan Harris.[275]

Brough Smyth wrote of Jonathan Harris' discovery that:

> "the reef was first opened by Jonathan Harris, in 1853; and in conjunction with the late Thos. Hustler – whose name the reef bears – they purchased a small claim on it, about twelve feet by twelve feet.
>
> The reef in the claim was remunerative from the surface downwards; and the first crushing yielded 26 ozs. per ton; and the rich specimens exhibited in the Melbourne Exhibition, in 1854, obtained for the proprietors a medal.
>
> Subsequently, the spirited holders of the small claim purchased several of the adjacent properties, and they finally obtained a lease of a considerable area."[276]

Brough Smyth's account appears for the most part to be accurate. However, as will be seen shortly, Jonathan did not purchase his claim in conjunction with Thomas Hustler. Rather Hustler purchased the claim from Jonathan and two others in 1854.[277]

In a number of publications, Jonathan Harris was said to have been "an African black": one of a party of African blacks who jointly discovered *Hustlers Reef*. The most expansive of such assertions is to be found in William Adcock's *The Gold Rushes of The Fifties*, published in 1912. In this work, Adcock first referred to Edward Emmett's discovery of gold-bearing quartz in Ironbark Gully in 1852 before continuing:

> "A year afterwards, a party of African blacks, run-away sailors who had deserted their ship for the attractions of the goldfields, struck the spot. They started to pitch their tent on the hill between Ironbark Gully and Commissioner's Gully, intending to sink for alluvial gold in the latter gully, but on clearing a space for their tent they found the surface, when they had cut down the thick scrub, plentifully strewed with rich quartz specimens and numberless loose pieces rugged gold, which they industriously collected. Abandoning for the time the search for alluvial gold, they heaped up the gold-bearing quartz, and, procuring hammers, pounded it and washed out considerable quantities of gold. They kept their operations secret for a time, but it became noticed in the neighbouring camps that the darkies lived very bountifully, and regaled themselves upon spirits bought by the case at the nearest store, and they were watched, and the handsome result of their primitive quartz crushing became known. They had, however, secured a legal title to the claim, and after they had opened the ground a few feet below the surface, and had obtained over 500 oz. of gold, they sold the claim to Mr. Hustler foe a few hundred pounds. He opened up the mine systematically, and made thousands of pounds profit in the first three months."[278]

Comparable assertions were made in an article published in the *Bendigo Advertiser* on 15 November 1912. The author of the article observed that:

---

275 See Robert Brough Smyth, *The Gold Fields and Mineral Districts of Victoria* (1869), p. 326.
276 *Ibid*.
277 See footnote 281 and the accompanying text below.
278 See William Adcock, *The Gold Rushes of The Fifties* (1912), p. 106. See also Whitelaw, *op. cit.*, p. 9; George Brown, *Bendigo Goldfield* (1936), p. 17; Flett, *op. cit.*, p. 48; Graeme Butler & Associates, *Eaglehawk & Bendigo Heritage Study: Significant Areas* (1993), Vol. 3, Appendix 1-2; and Cusack, *op. cit.*, p. 122.

"Gold was first discovered on the Hustler's line of reef in 1853 by Jonathan Harris, one of a numerous party of colored men who had found their way to the diggings, having probably deserted from some ship in port. When these men, who were African blacks, got the gold, they engaged in great rejoicings, and engaged a band to play on the claim. Subsequently they sold out to a party, included in whom were J. Hustler, a one-armed man, after whom the reef was called."[279]

The *Bendigo Advertiser* article inspired Jonathan Harris' three then-surviving sons (Jonathan William Harris, David Henry Harris and George Samuel Harris) to contact the newspaper both with a correction with respect to their father's origins and with intriguing biographical particulars relating to him. A summary of their contribution was published in the *Bendigo Advertiser* on 29 November 1912 as follows:

"Jonathan Harris was born in Sussex, England, and came to Australia when seven years old. He spent his younger days in Sydney, and from there he went to Tasmania, and was a detective in [the] police force. He captured one of the notorious bushrangers in Tasmania, and brought him 100 miles by coach to Hobart. He left that position and went to the California diggings, and was there some time, and came to Bendigo and started digging for alluvial. He and his wife kept a store on the Third White Hill. One morning he said to Mrs. Harris, 'I think I will take a walk to Eaglehawk'. He took a hammer with him, and on the way he came on a reef, now the old Hustler's, and the first piece he knocked off was covered with course gold. (We have the piece now). He worked the reef for some time, and then he got two American darkies to join him, and they worked it with gads and hammers, and got a lot of stuff out. There was no machinery to crush at that time, and he sold out to the American darkies; their names being Dunlop and Foster. He then went home to England and took several boxes of fine specimens with him. Some he sold in Melbourne, and what he took home he got crushed in England. In those days it was crushed through rollers instead of stampers, but the machinery being new, he lost a good bit of gold through it sticking to the rollers. He speculated in England in rum, which he purchased from Lemonheart's big spirit store in London. Returning to Australia, he started business in Melbourne. He was there for some time, but, not getting his health, he decided to take up land at Axedale. He died at Axedale on 20th July 1881. We have the baton which he had when [a] detective; also the Colt's revolver which he had in the mountains of California. In that country he saw stirring times. Besides encounters with grizzly bears and other things, he saw something of lynch law. Once he was in a fight on the diggers' side, the other side being the storekeepers. He got a couple of big bullets in his legs. Dr. Wall, a well-known Bendigonian, was the first man that landed Mr. Harris off the boat when he first came from England. Mrs. Harris died two years ago on Christmas Day at Axedale, aged 84 years."[280]

No doubt this account was constructed from anecdotes confided from time to time by Jonathan to his sons. One can only wonders how accurate its particulars were. It is noteworthy that the account made no mention

---

279   See the *Bendigo Advertiser*, Friday, 15 November 1912, p. 3
280   See the *Bendigo Advertiser*, Friday, 29 November 1912, p. 5. A "gad" was a wedge used with a hammer when hand-mining rock: see "Breaking Ore Underground" in *Cornish Mining WHS* (http://tinyurl.com/y4rrkn9q) (at 12 October 2020).

of Jonathan's conviction in 1842 or of his subsequent experiences as a convict in Van Diemen's Land. Perhaps Jonathan kept these to himself, or perhaps his sons simply chose not to mention them.

Jonathan's sons appear to have been in error in claiming that their father had sold his claim to the two American blacks: Dunlop and Foster. It seems more likely that after discovering the *Hustlers Reef* gold, Jonathan went on to form a working partnership with Dunlop and Foster and/or sold them a share in his claim; with the three men then selling their entitlements to Thomas Hustler in 1854.

The recollections of a miner named Louis Mason, who arrived at White Hills in Bendigo from Italy in early 1852, are significant here. In an article published in the *Bendigo Independent* on 5 June 1897, it was reported that:

> "Louis was asked by an Englishman named Harrison (sic), who then kept a store just below the Suburban Hotel on the White Hill road, and by two American niggers, one named Dunlop, a barber by trade, and the other was known as 'Bill' — Louis forgets his proper name, but his occupation was that of a parson — to buy a claim of theirs, they offered to part with it for one once of gold apiece. They showed several rich specimens but it being a quartz reef, Louis would not accept the offer. Eventually they persuaded Hustler to buy the claim."[281]

Louis Mason also had the following to say with respect to Jonathan's trip to London to mill his gold-bearing quartz:

> "Harrison (sic) before the claim was sold, took out a ton of quartz, and engaged 'Tom' Barrow, father of the late Mr. John Barrow, of the All Nations Hotel, Williamson street, to take it to Melbourne. Harrison (sic) then took it to London and had it treated, clearing £50 after all expenses had been paid."[282]

Finally with respect to Jonathan's activities as a miner in Bendigo, there can be no doubt but that he signed the Bendigo Goldfields Petition in 1853.[283]

Jonathan purchased his Axedale land at some point in time after 1853 and prior to 1860. Commencing in 1860, each of his five children (two of whom predeceased him) were born at Axedale.[284] Jonathan lived the balance of his life with his wife and surviving children on his farm. He died of the effects of hydatid disease on 20 July 1881, and was buried in the Axedale Cemetery on 23 July 1881.[285]

---

281 See the *Bendigo Independent*, Saturday, 5 June 1897, p. 2. See also James Lerk, *Bendigo's Mining History 1851-1954* (1991), p. 22. Thomas Hustler was born near Bradford, Yorkshire in 1814. Convicted of highway robbery in 1836, he was sentenced at the West Riding Quarter Sessions in Yorkshire in that year to be transported for seven years to Van Diemen's Land. After completing his sentence, he moved to the goldfields of Victoria. At some point in time, Hustler lost his left arm to the shoulder in a blasting accident. This did not stop him from becoming a prodigious digger: see *Convict Records – Thomas Hustler* (http://tinyurl.com/y7ztrl59) (at 4 March 2021); and the *Bendigo Independent*, Saturday, 29 May 1897, p. 2. Hustler was awarded a Bronze Medal after exhibiting a gold-impregnated quartz specimen at the Victorian Exhibition in Melbourne I 1854: see the *Victorian Government Gazette* (No. 19), Tuesday, 27 February 1855, p. 557. Interestingly, he was referred to in this Gazette as "Hussler, J, (Bendigo)": *Ibid*. Indeed, he was misnamed "Hussler" in a number of publications: see, for example, Adcock, *op. cit.*, p. 8. James Flett went so far as to erroneously refer to him as "the one-armed German, Thomas Hussler"): see Flett, *op. cit.*, p. 48. Hustler ultimately sold the *Hustlers Reef* claim to Jonathan Latham and John Watson in about 1857 or 1858: see the *Bendigo Independent*, Saturday, 5 June 1897, p. 2; and Flett, *op. cit.*, p. 48. Hustler died on 12 January 1863 and was buried in the Bendigo Cemetery: see *Tom Hustler – The One Armed Miner* (http://tinyurl.com/y7t7mr9f) (at 4 March 2021).
282 See the *Bendigo Independent*, Saturday, 5 June 1897, p. 2.
283 See footnote 233 and the accompanying text above.
284 See *Ancestry: Jonathan Harris Family Tree – Jonathan Harris* (http://tinyurl.com/yxh6butb) (at 12 October 2020).
285 See *Deaths in the District of Axedale, 1881 – Jonathan Harris* (No 6405/1881).

Elizabeth Clark (née Harris)

Jonathan Harris Snr's second child and eldest daughter, Elizabeth Clark (née Harris), was the first of Jonathan's children to marry. As mentioned above, Elizabeth married William Clark on 22 June 1839 in Bowning, New South Wales at the ripe old age of 15 years.[286]

Soon after her marriage, Elizabeth accompanied her new husband south across the Murray River to the squatting run he had established on the left bank of the Ovens River in what was then known as the Port Phillip District of New South Wales. William Clark had established his run there during 1838. He and Elizabeth set up their matrimonial in slab and bark hut William had constructed on the run at the top of the bank of the Ovens River. Over time, William came to call his run *Ovens Crossing Place*.

William Clark was of a decidedly entrepreneurial bent. Soon after Elizabeth arrived on the Ovens River, William acquired a shanty operated by Thomas Rattray; the first European to settle on the River near to its junction with the King River. At the same time, William also acquired Rattray's punt conveying people and goods across the Ovens River.

Over the course of his life, William Clark constructed and operated two local hotels: the *Hope Inn* and the *Commercial Hotel*. He also acquired interests in a flour mill, a brewery and a gold mine. However, his principal preoccupations were cattle grazing and property acquisitions. For a time, he held a squatting run of the King River which he named *Whitefield* (later *Whitfield*). In about 1849, land at the junction of the Ovens and King Rivers was excised from William's *Ovens Crossing Place* run as the site for the new town of Wangaratta. Over time, William purchased numerous freehold lots in and around Wangaratta; together with further allotments in Benalla and Bundalong.

Elizabeth and William Clark had 12 children together. Two of these children predeceased both of their parents.[287]

William Clark died of hepatitis and gall stones at Corowa in New South Wales on 24 April 1871. He was 61 years of age. Elizabeth was to survive him for over 17 years. She died in Wangaratta on Saturday, 29 September 1888 of "haemophysis and exhaustion". Following an Anglican burial service, she was interred in the Wangaratta Cemetery.[288]

An obituary published anonymously in the *Ovens and Murray Advertiser* on 13 October 1888 provides interesting insights into Elizabeth Clark's life and character:

---

286 See footnote 135 and the accompanying text above.
287 See *Ancestry: Jonathan Harris Family Tree – Elizabeth Harris* (http://tinyurl.com/y4dc6h3h) (at 13 October 2020); and *WikiTree – Elizabeth (Harris) Clark (abt. 1823-1888)* (http://tinyurl.com/mzuc78u) (at 13 October 2020).
288 See *Deaths in the District of Wangaratta, 1888 – Elizabeth Clark (No 16158/1888)*. "Haemophysis" is a haemorrhage in the lung caused by TB or other chronic pulmonary disease.

"I confess I was surprised that so little has been said in any of the district papers about the curious history and services of Mrs Clarke, of Wangaratta, recently deceased, widow of the late William Clarke, more familiarly and generally known as 'Old Bill Clarke' in the early days. Mrs Clarke, who was born in England, and came to Australia in her earliest youth, arrived in Wangaratta with her husband as far back as 1839, she being little more than 15 years of age. One solitary hut then represented the present township, and Clarke built a second one on the site of the present Sydney Hotel, now the property of Mr Painter, but facing towards the old cutting leading to the primitive punt which was also built and 'run' by him. This was of slab and bark, but he subsequently added a brick building to the hotel, facing, as Painter's does now, towards the present market. Here, when the Ovens rush took place, Mr Clarke, between the punt and the public-house, figuratively speaking, coined money, which he invested in property, and in building — after the bridge was finished — the Commercial Hotel, in Murphy-street, which is now a much more pretentious establishment. The writer of this was in those golden days a cadet in the police force — the troopers, as they were then called — and as the gold and prisoners' escorts always stopped at Mrs Clarke's, he had plenty of opportunities of knowing that lady and her kindly ways, and of hearing from others of the earlier part of her career in the district. It is of this latter I desire chiefly to speak. When Mrs Clarke settled in Wangaratta, there was not another woman in any direction within twenty miles; but she used to travel that distance on horseback on occasions, to comfort the sick or to help to bring little native Australians into the world, her own first child — she had twelve altogether — being the very first ever born in Wangaratta. All this was authenticated to me at a later date, although few now remain who witnessed it. But there are very many still living who stand to her almost in the light of foster-children, owing to her kind and charitable attention to their mothers in their need. I can speak personally of Mrs Clarke's friendly and pleasant ways when her family was growing more and more numerous, and I know that she made us fellows feel not only comfortable, but as if we were at home again. I write this because Mrs Clarke's many good qualities and great services — when such services were invaluable, and indeed, but for her, unprocurable — seem to be either unknown or forgotten."[289]

Four windows over the porch in Holy Trinity Cathedral, Wangaratta now commemorate the lives of Elizabeth and William Clark.[290]

---

289 See the *Ovens and Murray Advertiser*, Saturday, 13 October 1888, p. 6.
290 See the *Albury Banner and Wodonga Express*, Friday, 7 January 1910, p. 2. In 1860, William Clark donated land to the Anglican Church close to where the Cathedral now stands.

Henry Harris

Jonathan Harris' third child, Henry Harris, lived out at least the later part of his life in sad circumstances precipitated by a tragic incident.

Although born in Sussex, Henry grew up on the outskirts of Sydney and in the vicinity of Goulburn and the Tumut River in New South Wales. Little seems to be presently known of his adult life prior to 1863. It seems that he worked as a shearer. It is possible, but unlikely, that he married an Ann Hoskins in Geelong, Victoria on 3 March 1857.[291] If so, it is not currently known for how long they cohabited, or whether the marriage produced any children.[292]

On 1 December 1863, Henry Harris killed a Stephen Bonfield with a pair of sheep shears in the woolshed on Gobbagombolin Station near Wagga Wagga in New South Wales. A short while later, Henry was charged with Bonfield's murder.[293]

After being incarcerated in the Goulburn Gaol for nearly five months, Henry's mental fitness to stand trial for Bonfield's murder was tested on 26 April 1864 in a hearing before Mr Justice Milford and a Jury in the Supreme Court of New South Wales in Goulburn.

The overwhelming evidence called in the Supreme Court hearing on 26 April 1864 was to the effect that Henry was then insane, and violently insane to boot. Robert Waugh, a surgeon at the Goulburn Gaol, testified that Henry's conduct in prison:

> "had always been very violent, so much so that it was necessary to keep him constantly handcuffed and leg-ironed; he bit off a fellow prisoner's finger lately."[294]

Perhaps the most interesting evidence led at the fitness to plead hearing came from Henry's older brother, Jonathan Harris Jnr. Jonathan stated that:

> "I am a brother to [the] prisoner. He was confined in the asylum in Melbourne in 1854. He never

---

291 See *WikiTree – Henry Harris (1826-1904)* (http://tinyurl.com/y5habcrm) (at 14 October 2020). Ann Harris (née Hoskins) appears to have been born in Cashel, Tipperary in Ireland in about 1830: see *WikiTree – Ann Hoskins (abt. 1830-aft. 1857)* (http://tinyurl.com/y35u4v2t) (at 14 October 2020).

292 The *Jonathan Harris Family Tree* website asserts that Henry Harris married an Anne Hoskins in Victoria in 1857, and that the couple went on to have six children together in the Ballarat, Meredith and Lethbridge areas in that Colony between 1861 and 1873: see *Ancestry: Jonathan Harris Family Tree – Henry Harris* (http://tinyurl.com/y66y9rwv) (at 14 October 2020). However, it would seem that the Henry Harris who fathered six children with Anne Hoskins could not have been Jonathan Harris' son. From December 1863 until his death in 1904, Jonathan's son Henry, as will be seen below, was in the continuous custody of the New South Wales Government. The Ann or Anne Harris who married in Geelong in 1857 could well have married an unrelated Henry Harris. It might be noted that Geelong is reasonably close to Ballarat, and even closer to Meredith and Lethbridge.

293 See *The Empire (Sydney), Friday, 29 April 1864, p. 2.*

294 *Ibid.*

could be kept at home, but kept rambling about the country, and was always very violent in his manner. The certificate now produced of the prisoner's insanity, from the Melbourne Lunatic Asylum, was received by [me] on [my] brother's behalf. [I] did not see my brother for nine years, before the commission of the offence now charged against him. When about eight years of age, [the] prisoner got a sun-stroke at Tumut, and every summer since he has been very violent and unsettled in his mind."[295]

At the conclusion of the hearing, the Jury returned a verdict that Henry was then insane and mentally unfit to stand trial for Bonfield's murder. Pending further consideration of his mental state at a later date, he was confined in the Tarban Creek Mental Asylum at Gladesville in Sydney.[296]

In early October 1864, a determination was made that Henry Harris was then in a fit state of mind to stand trial for Bonfield's murder.[297] On 27 October 1864, that trial commenced before Mr Justice Wise and a Jury in the Supreme Court at Goulburn. Henry pleaded not guilty to the charge of wilfully murdering Bonfield. The principal evidence against him was led from another shearer, John Climes. Climes testified as follows:

"I am a shearer. On the 1st December, 1863, I was in the wool-shed working next [to the] prisoner. Sheahan was next [to] me. Bonfield was present, [and the prisoner] was there shearing. Bonfield had permission to shear. He wanted to learn. [The] prisoner said he should not learn. Bonfield replied, 'what is it to do with you?' [I] heard Bonfield tell [the] prisoner to shut up his gab. [The] prisoner said 'I will not'. Bonfield was leaning on the partition. Harris came close to me. I saw Harris strike Bonfield with the shears. When he stabbed him, [the] prisoner said, 'Ah, that's what you wanted long ago, you ----'. I saw only one blow. After [the] deceased was struck, he rushed out. Harris stepped back to his own place. I advised him to hang up his shears. I thought we should have a difficulty in getting them out of his hands. Harris went out. He was secured by the men."[298]

After deliberation for half an hour, the Jury delivered a verdict finding Harry guilty of Bonfield's murder. Mr Justice Wise then pronounced the sentence of death on him, and urged the necessity of repentance of his past misdeeds.[299]

It is interesting to note that notwithstanding the Jury's determination on 26 April 1864 that Henry was then mentally unfit to stand trial, Henry did not plead that he was not guilty of Bonfield's murder by reason of insanity. At the time of Henry's trial for the murder, the test for insanity as a defence to murder was that developed in Britain by the House of Lords in 1843 following the trial of Daniel McNaughton. The so-called *McNaughton Rules* mandated that in order to establish insanity as a defence to murder:

"It must be clearly proved that, at the time of committing the act, the party accused was labouring under

---

295 *Ibid*.
296 See the *Sydney Morning Herald*, Friday, 11 November 1864, p. 4. See also *Wikipedia – Gladesville Mental Hospital* (http://tinyurl.com/y29syw3t) (at 15 October, 2020).
297 See the *Sydney Morning Herald*, Wednesday, 5 October 1864, p. 4.
298 See the *Sydney Morning Herald*, Monday, 31 October 1864, p. 5.
299 *Ibid*. See also the *Sydney Morning Herald*, Friday, 28 October 1864, p. 5.

such a defect of reason, from disease of the mind, as not to know the nature and quality of the act he was doing, or, if he did know it, that he did not know he was doing what was wrong."[300]

One can only assume that Henry Harris' legal advisers concluded that their client would be unable to prove that he satisfied the requirements of the *McNaughton Rules* at the time he killed Bonfield. Nonetheless, it appears that it was clear to all that Henry was, and had been, mentally unwell. He was accordingly returned to the Tarban Creek Mental Asylum pending the New South Wales Government's further consideration of his fate.[301]

Finally, it was announced in *The Empire* on 2 December 1864 that:

"The sentence of death passed at the last Goulburn assizes on Henry Harris for the murder of Stephen Bonfield in the Wagga Wagga district, has been commuted to imprisonment for life, the first three years in irons. The commutation is owing to the presumed insanity of the convict, and it is not intended that the case shall be open to any further remission of the sentence."[302]

Henry Harris spent the balance of his life locked away in asylums. It would, indeed, be interesting to have an expert contemporary diagnosis of his mental pathology or pathologies. He died on Wednesday, 9 March 1904 in the Parramatta Hospital for the Insane.[303] He was 73 years of age when he died.

---

300 See *Wiktionary- McNaughton Rules* (http://tinyurl.com/y64unme5) (15 October 2020); and A Loughnan, *How the Insanity Defence Against a Murder Charge Works* (http://tinyurl.com/ybhdudxc) (at 15 October 2020).
301 See the *Sydney Morning Herald*, Friday, 11 November 1864, p. 4.
302 See *The Empire* (Sydney), Friday, 2 December 1864, p. 5.
303 See *Ancestry: Jonathan Harris Family Tree – Henry Harris* (http://tinyurl.com/y66y9rwv) (at 15 October 2020). See also State Records Authority of New South Wales, *Parramatta Hospital for the Insane* (http://tinyurl.com/y29vkjnw) (at 15 October 2020).

Sophia Fraser (née Harris)

Sophia Fraser (née Harris) was the fourth of Jonathan Harris' children and the first to be born in Australia.[304] She lived most of her long life in Goulburn and surrounding areas of New South Wales. Following her father's arrest and incarceration in 1842, she continued to live with her step-mother, Ann Harris (née Grubb), and other members of her own family, together with, or in close proximity to, members of Ann's family, at Murrays Flat to the immediate east of Goulburn.

On 15 May 1846, Sophia married a Joseph Young, a bachelor from Lockyersleigh, at Murrays Flat. The marriage was witnessed by Ann Harris' brother and sister-in-law, Thomas and Sarah Grubb.[305] Sophia was barely 14 years of age at the time of this marriage.

Sophia's marriage to Joseph Young appears to have been short-lived. In 1847, she gave birth to her first child whom she called Isabella Harris. In Isabella's Birth Registration Entry, the baby's father is named only as "William".[306]

In 1848, Sophia appears to have entered into a de facto relationship with John Povey.[307] The latter was born in Berkshire, England on 2 April 1809. On 16 July 1832, he was convicted of sheep stealing and sentenced to be transported to Australia. He received a Conditional Pardon in 1847.[308] It is not presently known what John's occupation was in Australia. However, it seems likely that he worked as an agricultural labourer.

Sophia and John Povey had a total of 11 children together, three of whom predeceased their mother.[309] On or a little before 12 April 1879, John himself died at Kippilaw, a short distance to the west of Goulburn.[310]

On 11 February 1883, Sophia married Alexander Fraser in North Goulburn.[311] She was then 51 years of age. Her new husband was 46 years old. Alexander Fraser was born in about 1837 in MacDuff, Banffshire in Scotland. He emigrated to Australia in 1876.[312] In Australia, he worked as a blacksmith. Alexander had no children with Sophia.

Alexander Fraser died on or about 19 June 1914 at the age of 77 years. He was buried in the Breadalbane

---

304 See footnote 110 and the accompanying text above.
305 See *Ancestry: Jonathan Harris Family Tree – Sophia Harris* (http://tinyurl.com/y4w6asl3) (at 17 October 2020); *WikiTree – Sophia (Harris) Fraser (1832-1926)* (http://tinyurl.com/y2ansqon) (at 17 October 2020); and *Ancestry – Sophia Harris in the Australia, Marriage Index, 1788-1950* (http://tinyurl.com/y932cgqg) (at 17 October 2020). See also footnote 141 and the accompanying text above.
306 See *WikiTree – Sophia (Harris) Fraser (1832-1926)*, Source Note 2 (http://tinyurl.com/y2ansqon) (at 17 October 2020). Isabella Harris was later known as Isabella Povey.
307 The *Jonathan Harris Family Tree* website asserts that Sophia in fact married John Povey at Bungonia east of Goulburn on 5 May 1848: see *Ancestry: Jonathan Harris Family Tree – Sophia Harris* (http://tinyurl.com/y4w6asl3) (at 17 October 2020). However, there would seem to be no record of Sophia divorcing Joseph Young or obtaining an annulment of her marriage to him. Nor would there appear to be any record of Sophia marrying John Povey. Interestingly, the *WikiTree* website for Sophia suggests that "Joseph Young" may have been a pseudonym used by John Povey: see *WikiTree – Sophia (Harris) Fraser (1832-1926)* (http://tinyurl.com/y2ansqon) (at 17 October 2020). Whilst this is possible, it appears to be entirely conjectural.
308 See *Ancestry: Jonathan Harris Family Tree – John Povey* (http://tinyurl.com/y328yd49) (at 17 October 2020).
309 See *Ancestry: Jonathan Harris Family Tree – Sophia Harris* (http://tinyurl.com/y4w6asl3) (at 17 October 2020).
310 See *Ancestry: Jonathan Harris Family Tree – John Povey* (http://tinyurl.com/y328yd49) (at 17 October 2020).
311 See *Ancestry: Jonathan Harris Family Tree – Sophia Harris* (http://tinyurl.com/y4w6asl3) (at 17 October 2020).
312 See *Ancestry: Jonathan Harris Family Tree – Alexander Fraser* (http://tinyurl.com/y6admejk) (at 17 October 2020).

Cemetery to the south-west of Goulburn.[313] Sophia Fraser died on Friday, 23 July 1926 at the home of one of her surviving daughters in Archer Street, Burwood in Sydney. She was 94 years old when she died. On Tuesday, 27 July 1826, she was buried in the grave of her late husband, Alexander Fraser, in the Breadalbane Cemetery.[314]

On 28 July 1926, the following obituary for Sophia Fraser was published in the *Goulburn Evening Penny Post*:

"**OVER 200 DESCENDANTS**

Breadalbane's Grand Old Lady

Late Mrs. Sophia Fraser

Mrs. Sophia Fraser, the grand old southern pioneer whose death was briefly noticed in the 'Post' on Monday, was born in Campbelltown 98 (sic) years ago.

There was probably no other resident of the Southern Tablelands with a greater fund of personal recollections. Her memories carried her back to the time when Goulburn consisted merely of a collection of bark-roofed humpies.

She was one of the earliest settlers in this district and had lived here practically all her life. Mrs. Fraser was a sterling type of Australian womanhood, and she leaves over 200 descendants.

She was twice married, her first husband being the late Mr. Povey. Her family comprised eight daughters and three sons, of whom five daughters and two sons are still living. The eldest daughter, Mrs North, is still hearty and is 79 years of age. Another surviving daughter id Mrs. Mary Morton, of Breadalbane. In addition, the deceased is survived by 46 grandchildren, 121 great-grandchildren, and 30 great-great-grandchildren.

A few years after her first husband's death, the deceased was married to Mr. Fraser, who predeceased her some time ago. There was no issue at all by the second marriage.

The late Mrs. Fraser had lived a great number of years at Breadalbane and had recently been residing at her daughter's residence at Burwood, where she died on Friday last.

The late Mrs Fraser used to relate numerous incidents in which the bushrangers. Gilbert, Hall, and Dunn, figured. On one occasion the out-laws called at the home of one of the deceased's neighbour's, Mrs. Humphreys, near Collector, and demanded food. They revealed their identity on leaving, and warned Mrs. Humphreys not to tell anyone for an hour afterwards that they had called. One of the party left some money on the kitchen table before leaving. Later the police called at the home of Mrs. Fraser (then Mrs. Povey) and enquired whether any of the gang had been seen.

The deceased's second husband, the late Mr. Alexander Fraser, followed the construction of the Cooma railway as a blacksmith. He also worked on the iron bridge at Gundagai. Mr. Walter Henry Wood, engine-driver, of Goulburn, is a grandson of the deceased.

Mrs. Fraser's body was brought from Sydney on Monday night by the Temora mail, and was interred in the Breadalbane cemetery in the presence of a large number of relatives and friends. The Rev. T. North, of Gunning, officiated."[315]

---

313   *Ibid.*
314   See *Ancestry: Jonathan Harris Family Tree – Sophia Harris* (http://tinyurl.com/y4w6asl3) (at 17 October 2020).
315   See the *Goulburn Evening Penny Post*, Wednesday, 28 July 1926, p. 6.

Thomas Harris

Jonathan Harris' fifth child, Thomas Harris, seems to have been a strong willed and somewhat eccentric man. He appears to have moved from the Goulburn area, where he grew up, to Victoria as a young adult. In, or a short while prior to, 1857, he was seemingly living in Wangaratta; perhaps in the home of his older sister, Elizabeth Clark (née Harris), and her husband, William Clark.[316]

On 20 February 1857, Thomas married Mary Ann Cook in St Paul's Anglican Church, Melbourne.[317] Thomas was 23 years old when they married. Mary Ann was 16 years of age. She was born in Goulburn in 1840; the daughter of Christopher Cook and Ellen Considine.[318] Mary Ann may have met Thomas Harris in Goulburn or, more likely, in Wangaratta, where she lived with her parents prior to her marriage.

At the time of his marriage to Mary Ann Cook, Thomas Harris worked as a carrier; probably operating with a horse and dray or other wagon.[319] It is likely that he continued to work as a carrier after his marriage. However, it is possible that inspired by his older brother, Jonathan Harris Jnr, he turned his hand to gold mining for a time as the first two of his 13 children were born in gold mining areas of Victoria: Ellen Harris in Pyalong in 1858, and Elizabeth Harris in Golden Square, Bendigo in 1860. In any event, after returning to Wangaratta, and then living in or around Gundagai for a time, Thomas moved with his family to the Bairnsdale district of Gippsland in about 1865. There, he spent most of the rest of his life.[320]

Tracing Thomas Harris' life in Gippsland through newspaper articles and other online documents is particularly difficult. The difficulty arises from the fact that two distinct Thomas Harrises seem to have lived partially overlapping lives in the Gippsland Lakes region: Jonathan Harris' son and another older, and apparently wilder, Thomas Harris. The latter was the subject of a brief biographical essay written in 2018 by Anna McNair.[321] Her Thomas Harris died of a burst aortic aneurism in 1889 when he was 78 years of age.[322] As will be seen below, Jonathan's Thomas Harris died in 1924 when he was 90 years old.

A number of newspaper references in the 1860s, 1870s and 1890s make it clear that McNair's Thomas Harris bore the nickname "Tom the Duck". By way of one example, the *Gippsland Times* reported the following prosecution brought in the Sale Police Court on 3 January 1865:

---

316 In his *Marriage Register Entry* in 1857, Thomas nominated Wangaratta as the place of his "usual residence": see *Victorian Marriage Register Entry, 1857 – Thomas Harris and Mary Ann Cook* (http://tinyurl.com/y5zla4pl and http://tinyurl.com/y38fm84c) (both at 19 October 2020).
317 Ibid.
318 See the *Moore Considine Family Tree – Cook, Mary Ann* (http://tinyurl.com/y5evdx54) (at 19 October 2020). Mary Ann Cook's maternal aunt, Margaret Considine, married John Moore in Goulburn in 1839. Mary Ann herself was a great-aunt of Sir John McEwan, Australia's 18th Prime Minister.
319 See *Victorian Marriage Register Entry, 1857 – Thomas Harris and Mary Ann Cook* (http://tinyurl.com/y5zla4pl and http://tinyurl.com/y38fm84c) (both at 19 October 2020).
320 See *Ancestry: Jonathan Harris Family Tree – Thomas Harris* (http://tinyurl.com/y4e3x9gq) (at 19 October 2020).
321 See Anna McNair, "Watermen of Gippsland" in (Dec. 2018) 8 *The PPM Journal* 7 (Published by the Paynesville Maritime Museum).
322 See McNair, op. cit., at p. 8. See also *Births, Deaths and Marriages, Victoria – Death Entry for Thomas Harris in 1889* (193/1889) (http://tinyurl.com/y22kom9p) (at 19 October 2020).

"First in order came Tom Harris ("Tom the Duck"), and son, charged with being drunk, disorderly, fighting, resisting the police, and tearing a constable's jumper. To these formidable charges, the elder and younger "ducks" pleaded New Year excesses. Verdict, 5/- fine each and £2 expenses for a new jumper for the constable."[323]

In 1865, Jonathan's Thomas Harris had only one son, Thomas Harris Jnr. The latter was then around two years old. There are a number of other newspaper reports which appear to clearly link "Tom the Duck" with McNair's Thomas Harris.

In her *Biography of Jonathan Harris*, Margaret Cooper has asserted that the Thomas Harris who was the son of Jonathan Harris was known as "Tom the Duck". It was, according to Cooper, a nickname he acquired by virtue of his "gurning", or face-pulling talents.[324] Whilst it is possible that the Bairnsdale district was fortunate enough to have two "Tom the Ducks" at the one time, it seems more likely that the nickname was borne only by McNair's Thomas Harris. If so, this would throw doubt on some of the biographical details in Cooper's essay.[325]

In any event, on reaching the Bairnsdale area, Thomas and Mary Ann Harris very likely established their home in Lucknow on the left bank of the Mitchell River, and just across that River from the village of Bairnsdale itself. The balance of their children appear to have been born in either Lucknow or Bairnsdale.[326] It could well be that Thomas continued working as a carrier. Given that fishing was a local industry, he may well have carted, as well as bought and sold, fish for a living.

Margaret Cooper, in her *Biography of Jonathan Harris*, provides two examples of Thomas Harris' eccentric behaviour which do not appear to be attributable to McNair's Tom the Duck. In the first place, Cooper's Thomas was reputed to be the only person able to climb a greased flagpole outside *Gingell's Club Hotel* in Bairnsdale.[327] However, perhaps his most audacious exploit was the part he played in the opening on 4 December 1875 of the first bridge across the Mitchell River linking Bairnsdale with Lucknow. In the words of Hal Porter:

"When the Sydney Harbour Bridge opening, in 1932, was unofficially done by Francis Edward de Groot, an antique dealer on horseback who slashed the ribbon with a sword before Premier J. T. Lang (whose wife, incidentally, was a Bairnsdale woman) could use the official scissors, it was because de Groot abhorred Lang's politics. His forerunner was at the Mitchell Bridge opening, though no one knows why Tom Harris, a fishmonger, wanted to circumvent the shire president and his scissors. Whipping up his horse, he drove his cart at the ribbon, and, trailing it, out of Bairnsdale's history. A grudge? For devilment? Drunk? Balmy? A glimpse is vouchsafed, and nothing more."[328]

According to Margaret Cooper, Thomas subsequently told family members that he had done what he did because he objected to the amount of money that had been wasted during the building of the bridge.[329]

---

323 See the *Gippsland Times*, Wednesday, 4 January 1865, p. 3.
324 See Cooper, *Biography of Jonathan Harris* (http://tinyurl.com/y6zb2kad) (at 19 October 2020)
325 According to McNair, her Tom the Duck had the ability to "swallow his face", and could hold a threepence between his nose and his chin. A composite photo of him doing so is currently held by the State Library of Victoria: see McNair, *op. cit.*, at p. 8. One part of this composite photo appears on the *Jonathan Harris Family Tree* website purporting to be a photo of Jonathan's Thomas: see *Ancestry: Jonathan Harris Family Tree – Thomas Harris* (http://tinyurl.com/yx9scpge) (at 19 October 2020). At the very least, it is possible that this photo is of McNair's Thomas Harris rather than of Jonathan Harris' fifth child.
326 See *Ancestry: Jonathan Harris Family Tree – Thomas Harris* (http://tinyurl.com/y4e3x9gq) (at 19 October 2020).
327 See Cooper, *Biography of Jonathan Harris* (http://tinyurl.com/y6zb2kad) (at 19 October 2020).
328 See Hal Porter, *Bairnsdale: Portrait of an Australian Country Town* (1977), p. 149
329 See Cooper, *Biography of Jonathan Harris* (http://tinyurl.com/y6zb2kad) (at 19 October 2020).

There was more to Thomas Harris than eccentric behaviour. An unnamed grandson recalled that Thomas was a very caring grandfather. Moreover, he was apparently well-known for his knowledge of horses; with people from all over the district bringing their horses to him "for treatment".[330]

On Wednesday, 9 May 1900, Mary Ann Harris died in the Alfred Hospital, Prahran of hemiplegia and exhaustion. Her hemiplegia was probably the result of a stroke. She was almost 60 years old when she died. Mary Ann was buried in the Bairnsdale Cemetery on Friday, 11 May 1900.[331]

It would appear that at some point in time prior to his death, Thomas Harris went to live with his eldest surviving daughter, Elizabeth Hewat, at 459 Rathdowne Street, North Carlton. He died there of senile decay and cardiac syncope at the age of 90 years on Thursday, 31 July 1924. Thomas was buried in the Bairnsdale Cemetery on Saturday, 2 August 1924.[332]

---

[330] Ibid.
[331] See *Ancestry: Jonathan Harris Family Tree – Mary Ann Cook* (http://tinyurl.com/yxvje2mg) (at 20 October 2020).
[332] See *Victorian Death Registry Entry, 1924 – Thomas Harris* (http://tinyurl.com/y4pdxrcn) (at 20 October 2020); *The Argus*, Friday, 1 August 1924, p. 1; and *Ancestry: Jonathan Harris Family Tree – Thomas Harris* (http://tinyurl.com/y4e3x9gq) (at 20 October 2020).

George Jarvis Harris

George Jarvis Harris was Jonathan Harris' sixth child. He was also the last of the children born of Jonathan's marriage to his first wife, Elizabeth Harris (née Baker).

Like his older brother, Thomas Harris, George Jarvis Harris apparently moved from the Goulburn district in New South Wales to Victoria as a young adult during the first half of the 1850s. And like Thomas, it seems that he initially moved to Wangaratta, where his older sister, Elizabeth Clark (née Harris), was living with her husband, William Clark, and their young family.[333]

On 27 August 1856, George married Annie Matilda Brown in St Mark's Anglican Church, Collingwood. The official witnesses to the marriage were George's oldest brother, Jonathan Harris Jnr, and the latter's wife, Harriet Harris. At the time of the marriage, George was said to be working as a carrier.[334]

Annie Matilda Harris (née Brown) was born at Newry in County Down, Ireland; the daughter of George and Suzannah Brown. There is some uncertainty surrounding the date of Annie's birth. However, the most likely year was 1834.[335] She probably arrived in Wangaratta with her parents in about 1849.[336] At the time of her marriage to George Jarvis Harris, her father was seemingly employed as a clerk.[337]

Why George and Annie Harris married in Collingwood is unknown. Perhaps George had found employment as a carrier in Melbourne. In any event, it would seem that the newly-married couple soon returned to Wangaratta, where their first child, Georgina Annie Harris, was born in 1857.[338]

Just as there is some uncertainty as to Annie Harris' year of birth, so there would seem to be a measure of doubt surrounding the number of children she had with George Jarvis Harris. The *Grandfather Mystery Tree* website, which appears to be arguably the most reliable in this respect, asserts that there were 10 children in all; at least four of whom predeceased Annie.[339] In contrast, the *Jonathan Harris Family Tree* website lists a total of nine children.[340] Most of these children seem to have been born in Benalla.[341] It appears likely that George,

---

333 George Jarvis Harris' *Marriage Register Entry* records that his place of "usual residence" in 1856 was Wangaratta: see *Victorian Marriage Register Entry, 1856 – George Jarvis Harris and Annie Matilda Brown* (http://tinyurl.com/y2zrc5jl) (at 23 October 2020).

334 *Ibid*.

335 In her *Marriage Register Entry*, Annie's age was said to be 22 years: *Ibid*. This would place her birth in 1834. However, in her *Death Register Entry*, her age at death in 1874 was given as 37 years: see *Deaths in the District of Wangaratta, 1874 – Annie Harris* (No. 12209/1874). If correct, this would mean that she was born in 1837. Arguably, the *Marriage Register Entry* is likely to have been more reliable than the *Death Register Entry*.

336 Annie's *Death Register Entry* recorded that she had lived in Victoria for 25 years prior to her death in 1874: see *Deaths in the District of Wangaratta. 1874 – Annie Harris* (No. 12209/1974).

337 See *Victorian Marriage Register Entry, 1856 – George Jarvis Harris and Annie Matilda Brown* (http://tinyurl.com/y2zrc5jl) (at 23 October 2020).

338 See *Ancestry: Grandfather Mystery Tree – Annie Matilda Brown* (http://tinyurl.com/y5ljrqqc) (at 23 October 2020).

339 *Ibid*.

340 See *Ancestry: Jonathan Harris Family Tree – Annie Matilda Brown* (http://tinyurl.com/y5enu9up) (at 23 October 2020).

341 See *Ancestry: Grandfather Mystery Tree – Annie Matilda Brown* (http://tinyurl.com/y5ljrqqc) (at 23 October 2020). However, it should be noted that at least two of George and Annie Harris' 10 children appears to have been born in Wangaratta, one in Glenrowan and one in Lucknow (where George's brother, Thomas Harris, was then living): *Ibid*.

Annie and their family were living in Benalla or its environs from no later than 1859 onwards. Benalla, of course, was by then the home of George's father, Jonathan Harris.

On 16 October 1874, Annie Harris died in the Wangaratta Hospital. The official cause of her death was said to be "phthisis" (tuberculosis of the lungs). It was noted that she had been suffering from this disease for some six months before she died. Annie was buried in the Wangaratta Cemetery on 17 October 1874.[342]

At some point in time prior to 1877, George Jarvis Harris began a relationship with Jane Molina Moore (née Dawson). That relationship was to endure until George's death in 1928.[343]

Jane Dawson was born on 17 December 1852 at Denham Court near Campbelltown in New South Wales; the daughter of Isaac and Isabella Dawson. At the time of Jane's birth, Isaac was described as being a farmer. Jane was christened in St Mary the Virgin's Anglican Church, Denham Court on 23 January 1853.[344]

On 19 September 1870, Jane Dawson married Charles Moore in St Saviour's Anglican Church, Goulburn.[345] Where and how Jane met Charles, and why they married in Goulburn, are presently uncertain. Charles Moore was born on or shortly prior to 24 August 1849 at the Ovens River in Victoria; the fourth surviving child of John Moore and his wife, Margaret Moore (née Considine).[346]

Irrespective of why they might have married in Goulburn, Charles and Jane Moore established their matrimonial home or homes in North Eastern Victoria. One of their three children was born in Taminick. The remaining two were born in Wangaratta; with the last, Richard Isaac Moore, only living for a short time in 1875.[347] The nature of Charles' occupation is currently unknown. However, it seems likely that he worked throughout as an agricultural labourer.

Whether Charles Moore abandoned Jane or Jane left Charles for George Jarvis Harris remains unclear. Jane and George probably met in or around Wangaratta. In any event, it could well have been that Jane and Charles' separation and/or Jane's new relationship with George precipitated something of a scandal in the Wangaratta community of the time. For whatever cause, Jane and George appear to have left Victoria soon after they began cohabiting. They both lived the rest of their lives in New South Wales.[348]

In New South Wales, Jane became known as Jane Harris. Her *Death Certificate* states that she married George Jarvis Harris in Echuca when she was 28 years of age.[349] If correct, this would mean that the marriage probably occurred in 1880. However, as the *Moore Considine Family Tree* website points out, there would seem to be no record of a divorce between Jane and Charles Moore, or of a marriage between Jane and George Jarvis Harris.[350] It seems likely, therefore, that George and Jane enjoyed a de facto relationship.

---

342 See *Deaths in the District of Wangaratta, 1874 – Annie Harris* (No. 12209/1874).

343 Jane Molina Moore's last child with her husband Charles Moore, Richard Isaac Moore, was born in Wangaratta in 1875. Her first child with George Jarvis Harris, Elizabeth Jane Harris, was born in Wagga Wagga on or a little before 9 July 1877: see *Ancestry: Jonathan Harris Family Tree – Jane Molina Dawson* (http://tinyurl.com/yxoepm4f) (at 23 October 2020). It therefore seems likely that George began cohabiting with Jane in 1876.

344 See *Ancestry – Sydney, Australia, Anglican Parish Registers, 1814-2011 for Jane Dawson* (http://tinyurl.com/yydh7jey) (at 23 October 2020).

345 See *Ancestry – Australian Marriage Index, 1788-1950 for Jane Dawson* (http://tinyurl.com/ybcjsmox) (at 23 October 2020). See also *Ancestry: Jonathan Harris Family Tree – Jane Molina Dawson* (http://tinyurl.com/yxoepm4f) (at 23 October 2020).

346 See *Ancestry: Jonathan Harris Family Tree – Charles Moore* (http://tinyurl.com/y5vxa4ly) (at 23 October 2020). See also footnote 318 above.

347 See *Ancestry: Jonathan Harris Family Tree – Charles Moore* (http://tinyurl.com/y5vxa4ly) (at 23 October 2020).

348 See *Ancestry: Jonathan Harris Family Tree – George Jarvis Harris* (http://tinyurl.com/yyqhxe4a) (at 23 October 2020); and *Ancestry: Jonathan Harris Family Tree – Jane Molina Dawson* (http://tinyurl.com/yxoepm4f) (at 23 October 2020). It would seem that Charles Moore had no further romantic entanglements following the breakdown of his marriage to Jane. He certainly appears to have had no further children. Charles died at Edi on the King River on 21 August 1929: see *Ancestry: Jonathan Harris Family Tree – Charles Moore* (http://tinyurl.com/y5vxa4ly) (at 23 October 2020).

349 See *New South Wales Death Certificate, 1933 – Jane Harris* (http://tinyurl.com/yyjclabu) (at 23 October 2020). See also *Ancestry: Jonathan Harris Family Tree – Jane Molina Dawson* (http://tinyurl.com/yxoepm4f) (at 23 October 2020). The *Jonathan Harris Family Tree* website also asserts that the marriage may have occurred at Echuca in 1876: *Ibid*.

350 See the *Moore Considine Family Tree – Charles Moore* (http://tinyurl.com/y27lc2ws) (at 23 October 2020).

George and Jane Harris spent most of their lives together in the south-east of New South Wales. Between 1877 and 1896, they had a total of 10 children together. Three were born in Wagga Wagga, two in Young, two in Junee and one in each of Temora, Wyalong and Adelong.[351] Of all Jonathan Harris' children, George Jarvis Harris gave him the most grandchildren. It should also be said that there seems to have been an element of narcissism associated with the names George saw fit to give to his own children: Georgina, George, Georgetta, Georgethel and Georgie.[352]

George Jarvis Harris died at Kogarah in Sydney on Tuesday, 26 June 1928. He was subsequently buried in the Rookwood Cemetery.[353] Jane Harris died of chronic myocarditis at Glebe in Sydney on Sunday, 10 December 1933. On Tuesday, 12 December 1933, she was buried in George's grave in the Rookwood Cemetery.[354]

---

[351] See *Ancestry: Jonathan Harris Family Tree – Jane Molina Dawson* (http://tinyurl.com/yxoepm4f) (at 23 October 2020).

[352] See *Ancestry: Jonathan Harris Family Tree – George Jarvis Harris* (http://tinyurl.com/yyqhxe4a) (at 23 October 2020).

[353] Ibid.

[354] See *New South Wales Death Certificate, 1933 – Jane Harris* (http://tinyurl.com/yyiclabu) (at 23 October 2020); and *Ancestry: Jonathan Harris Family Tree – Jane Molina Dawson* (http://tinyurl.com/yxoepm4f) (at 23 October 2020). See also the *Sydney Morning Herald*, Tuesday, 12 December 1933, p. 7.

William Thomas Harris

William Thomas Harris was the seventh of Jonathan Harris' children, and the first born to Jonathan's second wife, Ann Harris (née Grubb).

William Harris was not yet one year's old when his father was arrested in August 1842 for robbing Alfred King.[355] It is almost certain that Jonathan would never have seen William again thereafter.

Together with his younger brother, George Robert Grubb Harris, William grew up in and around Goulburn with his mother, her new partner, William Olliver, and their four children.[356] It seems likely that William Olliver treated the young William Harris and George Robert Grubb Harris as his own sons, and that they, in turn, treated him as their father. However, it is clear that by the time William Harris married in 1865, he was aware of his true parentage.[357]

William Olliver was a baker and confectioner by trade. In 1861, he moved to the Burrangong goldfield near Young in New South Wales. He was accompanied there by his family, including William Harris. Whether William Olliver worked on the goldfield as a baker or as a prospector is not presently known. However, William Harris, who was then 19 or 20 years of age, apparently did try his hand at prospecting for gold at the goldfield.[358]

The Olliver family's time on the Burrangong goldfield coincided with the notorious anti-Chinese Lambing Flat Riots.[359] However, it is not known whether either William Olliver or William Harris were involved in any of the riots. In any event, the Olliver family's residence on the goldfield seemingly ended with Ann Olliver's death on 30 December 1861. Following Ann's burial in the Young Cemetery, they returned to the Goulburn district.[360]

On 10 August 1865, William Harris married Ann Hutchings in the Wesleyan Chapel at Murrays Flat near Goulburn. The official witnesses to the marriage were William's half-sister, Elizabeth Ann Olliver, and his uncle, Thomas Grubb.[361]

Ann Harris (née Hutchings) was born on or shortly before 3 January 1842 in Huntsham, Devon in England.[362] She was the daughter of William Hutchings and his wife, Ann Hutchings (née Morgan). It is not presently known when the Hutchings family immigrated to Australia. However, on his daughter's *Marriage Certificate*, William

---

355 See footnote 146 and the accompanying text above.
356 See footnote 219 and the accompanying text above.
357 See *Ancestry – Marriage Certificate for William Thomas Harris and Ann Hutchings, 1865* (http://tinyurl.com/y2ct95on) (at 24 October 2020).
358 See William Harris' obituary in the *Goulburn Evening Penny Post*, Thursday, 15 May 1913, p. 2.
359 See *Wikipedia – Lambing Flat Riots* (http://tinyurl.com/y6hvz4y4) (at 24 October 2020).
360 See footnote 222 and the accompanying text.
361 See *Ancestry – Marriage Certificate for William Thomas Harris and Ann Hutchings, 1865* (http://tinyurl.com/y2ct95on) (at 24 October 2020).
362 See *Ancestry: Jonathan Harris Family Tree – Ann Hutchings* (http://tinyurl.com/y24vzp5j) (at 24 October 2020).

Hutchings was described as a farmer.[363] It is likely that he was farming in the Goulburn district when Ann met William Harris.

Between 1866 and 1885, Ann Harris gave birth to a total of 15 children. At least seven of these children predeceased William Harris. No less than eight died prior to the death of Ann Harris.[364]

In his *Marriage Certificate*, William Harris' occupation was given as "farmer".[365] Whether he owned or was renting a farm at the time of his marriage is not currently known. It is possible that he made enough money on the Burrangong goldfield to enable him to purchase land on which to farm. However, this is pure speculation. What does not appear to be speculative is that William in later life became a substantial orchardist; with his orchard being located in or around North Goulburn.[366]

Unfortunately, things ultimately did not go well for William's orchard business. On 4 July 1893, he was declared bankrupt in the Supreme Court of New South Wales on his own Petition.[367] It may be that the Great Depression of the early 1890s contributed to Williams insolvency. On Monday, 1 October 1894, William was ordered in the Goulburn Police Court to deliver a horse, a cart and two cows to an Alfred Norman. Over William's objections, Norman successfully argued in Court that he had purchased the cart and animals from William's bankrupt estate.[368] Following his bankruptcy, William appears to have been employed as a gardener – presumably growing vegetables to market.[369]

William Harris died at his home in North Goulburn on Thursday, 15 May 1913. He was then 71 years old. He was subsequently buried in the Goulburn Cemetery.[370] In its obituary for William, the *Goulburn Evening Penny Post* wrote:

> "Mr. William Thomas Harris died at his residence, Union-street, North Goulburn, this (Thursday) morning at the age of 72 (sic), the cause of death being old age. Mr. Harris was born in Auburn-street, and has lived here practically all his life. He was one of the oldest Goulburn natives alive. In his early days he was a prospector, and knew Lambing Flat and other diggings. He would tell many stories of those exciting times, and knew every incident of the bushranging days. Later in life he settled down as an orchardist, and carried on a large business at one time in Goulburn. Had he lived till September he would have celebrated his golden wedding. He leaves a widow, five sons, and two daughters. The sons are William (Albury), Walter (Bungonia), Thomas (Goulburn), Arthur A. G. (Wollongong), and J. J. Harris (Moss Vale). The daughters are Mrs. Thomas Gransell (Goulburn) and Mrs. G. Brockbury (Queanbeyan). He is survived by 25 grandchildren."[371]

Ann Harris died on Sunday, 11 June 1922 in Goulburn. She was 80 years of age when she died, and was buried in her husband William's grave in the Goulburn Cemetery.[372]

---

363 See *Ancestry – Marriage Certificate for William Thomas Harris and Ann Hutchings, 1965* (http://tinyurl.com/y2ct95on) (at 24 October 2020).

364 See *Ancestry: Jonathan Harris Family Tree – William Thomas Harris* (http://tinyurl.com/y53d9gzg) (at 24 October 2020); and *Ancestry: Jonathan Harris Family Tree – Ann Hutchings* (http://tinyurl.com/y24vzp5j) (at 24 October 2020).

365 See *Ancestry – Marriage Certificate for William Thomas Harris and Ann Hutchings, 1865* (http://tinyurl.com/y2ct95on) (at 24 October 2020).

366 See William Harris' obituary in the *Goulburn Evening Penny Post*, Thursday, 15 May 1913, p. 2.

367 See *New South Wales Government Gazette* (No.495), Friday, 14 July 1893, p. 5478.

368 In Court, William had unsuccessfully argued that Norman had agreed to buy the property in question from the bankrupt estate for William and one of his sons in return for vegetables to be delivered by the unnamed son to Norman: see the *Goulburn Herald*, Monday 1 October 1894, p. 2.

369 See *Ancestry: Australian Electoral Roll for North Goulburn, 1913 – William Thomas Harris* (http://tinyurl.com/yxszwscz) (at 24 October 2020).

370 See *Ancestry: Jonathan Harris Family Tree – William Thomas Harris* (http://tinyurl.com/y53d9gzg) (at 24 October 2020).

371 See the *Goulburn Evening Penny Post*, Thursday, 15 May 1913, p. 2.

372 See *Ancestry: Jonathan Harris Family Tree – Ann Hutchings* (http://tinyurl.com/y24vzp5j) (at 25 October 2020).

George Robert Grubb Harris

George Robert Grubb Harris was Jonathan Harris' eighth child. He was also the second and last child born of Jonathan's marriage to his second wife, Ann Harris. Whereas George's older brother, William Thomas Harris, was born a little under a year before Jonathan's arrest in August 1842 and subsequent transportation to Van Diemen's Land, George was born some eight months after that arrest. There is some sadness in the realisation that George and Jonathan probably never laid eyes on one another.

Together with his brother William, George grew up in and around Goulburn in a household largely comprised of his mother, her new partner, William Olliver, and their four children. Although he was christened in St Saviour's Church, Goulburn in April 1843 as George Robert Grubb Harris[373], he was seemingly raised believing that he was an Olliver, and that William Olliver was his biological father. Indeed, it appears that he was baptised a second time at Gunning near Goulburn on 5 November 1848, and on that occasion his parents were said to be William and Ann Olliver.[374]

William Olliver was a baker and confectioner by trade, and George evidently followed in his step-father's footsteps. During the 1850s, George almost certainly worked in William Olliver's Goulburn bakery.[375]

During 1861, the Olliver family, including George, moved to the Burrangong goldfield near Young. It is not presently known whether William Olliver worked as a baker or as a prospector on the goldfield. However, it seems that George's brother, William Harris, did prospect there, and it appears equally likely that George did so too.

Ann Olliver died on the Burrangong goldfield on 30 December 1861 and was buried in the nearby Young Cemetery.[376] Thereafter, most of the Olliver family appear to have returned to Goulburn. However, George (and perhaps his brother William) may have remained on the goldfield a little longer. On 30 May 1863, a George Olliver married a Susan Whittaker on the Ten Mile goldfield at Young.[377]

If the George Olliver who married Susan Whittaker at Young was in fact George Robert Grubb Harris, the couple did not appear to live together for long. On 28 June 1864, George married Bridget Burren at Towrang; a locality to the north-east of Goulburn. The *Marriage Certificate* recorded that George was 21 years old and then

---

373   See footnote 161 and the accompanying text above.
374   Ibid.
375   See Anon., "George Robert Grubb Harriss" in *Ancestry: Foster-Wood Family Tree – George Robert Grubb Harriss* (http://tinyurl.com/y5g9fnhj) (at 25 October 2020).
376   See footnote 222 and the accompanying text above.
377   See *Ancestry: Australia, Marriage Index, 1788-1950 – Susan Whittaker* (http://tinyurl.com/y5ecw77r) (at 25 October 2020). See also Anon., "George Robert Grubb Harriss" in *Ancestry: Foster-Wood Family Tree – George Robert Grubb Harris* (http://tinyurl.com/y5g9fnhj) (at 25 October 2020).

living at Towrang. He was said to be a baker by occupation. The official witnesses to the marriage were George's brother, William Harris, and a neighbour from Murrays Flat, Sarah Ann Erby.[378]

By the time of his marriage to Bridget Burren, George was aware that he was not in fact the biological son of William Olliver. From then on, he used his real father's surname as his own (although sometimes adding an extra "s" at the end of the name). George further appears to have dropped "Grubb" as one of his middle names.[379]

Bridget Burren was born on or a little before 29 December 1845 at Appin, to the south-east of Campbelltown on the outskirts of Sydney.[380] She was the daughter of Stephen and Johannah Burren.[381] Stephen Burren's occupation is not currently known. However, it is likely that he was either a farmer or a farm labourer in the Goulburn district at the time of his daughter's marriage to George.

It would appear that George worked as a baker for the balance of his working life. He may well have initially taken over William Olliver's bakery in Goulburn from the latter.[382] In any event, it would seem that he pursued the baker's trade at bakeries in Goulburn, Yass, Wagga Wagga and finally Parramatta.[383]

George and Bridget Harris had a total of 12 children together. Three of these children were born in Goulburn, three in Yass, four in Wagga Wagga and two in Parramatta. A total of four of the children predeceased both of their parents.[384]

In early 1910, George and Bridget Harris were living at 19 Mary Street, Surry Hills in Sydney. George died there on Monday, 31 January 1910. He was 66 years old when he died. George was buried in the Rookwood Cemetery on Wednesday, 2 February 1910.[385]

Bridget Harris died at Waterloo in Sydney on Friday, 27 May 1927 at the age of 81 years. She was subsequently buried with her late husband George in the Rookwood Cemetery.[386]

---

378 See *Ancestry: Australia, Marriage Index, 1788-1950 – George R Harriss* (http://tinyurl.com/y3r6g6sz) (at 25 October 2020); *Ancestry : Jonathan Harris Family Tree – George Robert Grubb Harris* (http://tinyurl.com/y4eol8y8) (at 25 October 2020); and Anon., "George Robert Grubb Harriss" in *Ancestry: Foster Wood Family Tree – George Robert Grubb Harriss* (http://tinyurl.com/y5g9fnhj) (at 25 October 2020). If George Harris had in fact married Susan Whittaker at Young on 30 May 1863, his subsequent marriage to Bridget Burren at Towrang on 28 June 1864 would have been bigamous. The issue merits further research.

379 See, for example, *Ancestry: Australia, Marriage Index 1788-1950 – George R Harriss* (http://tinyurl.com/y3r6g6sz) (at 25 October 2020).

380 See *Ancestry: Jonathan Harris Family Tree – Bridget Burren* (http://tinyurl.com/y4h7erw3) (at 25 October 2020).

381 See *Ancestry: New South Wales Births, Deaths and Marriages – Birth Entry for Bridget Burren* (No. 253/1845).

382 See Anon., "George Robert Grubb Harriss" in *Ancestry: Foster-Wood Family Tree – George Robert Grubb Harriss* (http://tinyurl.com/y5g9fnhj) (at 25 October 2020).

383 See *Ancestry: Jonathan Harris Family Tree – George Robert Grubb Harris* (http://tinyurl.com/y4eol8y8) (at 25 October 2020).

384 *Ibid.* See also *Ancestry: Jonathan Harris Family Tree – Bridget Burren* (http://tinyurl.com/y4h7erw3) (at 25 October 2020).

385 See *Ancestry: Jonathan Harris Family Tree – George Robert Grubb Harris* (http://tinyurl.com/y4eol8y8) (at 25 October 2020); *Ancestry: Australia, Death Index 1787-1985 – George R Harris* (http://tinyurl.com/y6k9lt4f) (at 25 October 2020); and the *Sydney Morning Herald*, Wednesday, 2 February 1910, p. 16.

386 See *Ancestry: Jonathan Harris Family Tree – Bridget Burren* (http://tinyurl.com/y4h7erw3) (at 25 October 2020); and the *Sydney Morning Herald*, Saturday, 26 May 1928, p. 19.

Edward Harris

Edward Harris was the nineth of Jonathan Harris' children, and the first of nine to be born to Jonathan's third wife, Mary Ann Harris (née Squire). Like his younger brother Walter, Edward was born in Hobart. When Jonathan and Mary Ann Harris, together with Edward and Walter, first arrived in Benalla in 1856, Edward was two years old.[387] Edward was to live the balance of his life in Benalla.

On his *Marriage Certificate*, Edward Harris was said to be a labourer by occupation.[388] During his early years, it seems likely that Edward would have assisted his father with Jonathan Harris' market garden. It appears that this was located in part on the land Jonathan had purchased in 1858 in Edward's name in Market Street, Benalla, and in part on the land in nearby Garden Street which Jonathan had acquired in his own name in 1860.[389] However, it would seem that Edward worked as a carrier in later life.[390]

On 23 April 1878, Edward Harris married Johanna O'Brien in the Holy Trinity Anglican Church in Wangaratta. Edward was 24 years old at the time of the marriage: Johanna was 21 years of age. The official witnesses to the marriage were Edward's parents, Jonathan and Mary Ann Harris.[391]

Johanna O'Brien was born on 16 June 1857 in Nunawading; then a rural district to the east of Melbourne. She was the third child of John O'Brien and his wife, Johanna O'Brien (née Finn). John and Johanna O'Brien were originally from County Tipperary in Ireland. At the time of Johanna O'Brien Jnr's birth, her father was apparently working as a labourer in the Nunawading area.[392]

At some time after the birth of Johanna's younger brother, John O'Brien at Nunawading in 1865, her parents moved with Johanna and her siblings to the Benalla district.[393] There, her father apparently took up a farm.[394] It seems likely that Edward Harris first met Johanna in or around Benalla.

Edward and Johanna Harris probably lived their entire married lives in a house constructed on the land in

---

387 See footnote 228 and the accompanying text above.
388 See *Ancestry – Marriage Certificate for Edward Harris and Johanna O'Brien, 1878* (http://tinyurl.com/yxruyrg3) (at 26 October 2020).
389 See footnotes 237 and 240, together with their accompanying texts, above.
390 See *Ancestry: Deaths in the District of Benalla, 1934 – Edward Harris* (http://tinyurl.com/y4oyua7s) (at 26 October 2020).
391 See *Ancestry – Marriage Certificate for Edward Harris and Johanna O'Brien, 1878* (http://tinyurl.com/yxruyrg3) (at 26 October 2020). Interestingly, Edward's younger sister, Charlotte Rebecca Harris, was to marry Johanna's younger brother, John O'Brien, in Benalla on 24 December 1888: see *Ancestry: Jonathan Harris Family Tree – Charlotte Rebecca Harris* (http://tinyurl.com/y2oh29wz) (at 26 October 2020). See also Cooper, *Biography of Jonathan Harris* (http://tinyurl.com/y6zb2kad) (at 26 October 2020).
392 See *Ancestry: Births in the District of Collingwood, 1857 – Johanna O'Brien* (http://tinyurl.com/y5vjbv52) (at 26 October 2020). Although Johanna was born in Nunawading, her birth was registered for some currently unknown reason in Collingwood: Ibid. See also *Ancestry: Johannah Obrien in the Australia, Birth Index 1788-1922* (http://tinyurl.com/y2d9gz59) (at 26 October 2020).
393 See *Ancestry: Jonathan Harris Family Tree – John O'Brien* (http://tinyurl.com/y6j6hvl4) (at 26 October 2020).
394 See the obituary for Edward Harris in the *North Eastern Ensign*, Friday, 16 March 1934, p. 3; and *Ancestry – Death Certificate for Johanna Harris* (http://tinyurl.com/y4v8st7t) (at 26 October 2020).

Market Street, Benalla acquired by Jonathan in Edward's name.[395] They had a total of seven children together.[396] Over the course of his life, Edward appears to have been a popular man in Benalla. Part of his popularity may have been due to his fondness for, and skills in, sporting pursuits.

Edward Harris died at his home of the effects of diabetes on Tuesday, 13 March 1934. It would seem that at some time prior to his death, he had converted from Anglicanism to Catholicism. Edward was buried in the Catholic section of the Benalla Cemetery on Wednesday, 14 March 1934.[397] In its obituary, the *North Eastern Ensign* observed:

> "One of the oldest and most highly respected residents of Benalla, in the person of Mr Edward Harris, passed away on Tuesday last at his residence in Garden Street, at the age of 80 years. He arrived in Benalla from Tasmania at the age of two years and during his long association with the district his bright and happy manner brought him many friends. He was one of the fine old pioneers who was always noted for his sterling qualities. He took a keen interest in many sports gatherings for years and being a great runner in his day, he was a leading figure and won several important events. At the age of 24 years he married Miss Johanna O'Brien, of Wangaratta, and for the past 56 years he resided in Benalla West. He was noted for his kind heartedness and many of his old friends will regret to hear of his demise. Deep sympathy is felt for his bereaved wife and family, viz., Hilda (Mrs Doherty, Melbourne), Jack (Mansfield), Ethel (Benalla), Frances (Mrs Goulding, Yarrawonga) and Maggie (Mrs Danaher, Wodonga). The remains were conveyed to the Benalla cemetery for interment, a large number of mourners following the cortege. The coffin bearers were Messrs R. Doherty (Melbourne), W. Crimmins, J. Quinn, T. Tanner, A. V. Ikin and L. Brennan, and the pall bearers were Messrs J. J. Doherty, J. O'Brien (Melbourne), J. Harris, T. Symons, W. Reynolds and E. Cherry. Rev. Father O'Reilly read the burial service, whilst the mortuary arrangements were carried out by Mr T. Connolly."[398]

Johanna Harris died of heart failure and a cerebral haemorrhage on 24 January 1945 at her home in Benalla. She was 86 years of age when she died, and was buried in Edward's grave at the Benalla Cemetery on 25 January 1945.[399] Sadly, she was predeceased by five of her seven children.[400]

---

395 Johanna Harris' *Death Certificate* stated that she died in Market Street, Benalla: *Ibid*. It might be noted that in Edward Harris' obituary in the *North Eastern Ensign*, Edward was said to have been living in Garden Street, Benalla when he died: see the *North Eastern Ensign*, Friday, 16 March 1934, p. 3. Market and Garden Streets run in parallel close to one another. It may well be that the author of the obituary was mistaken about the address of the house.

396 See *Ancestry: Jonathan Harris Family Tree – Edward Harris* (http://tinyurl.com/y6jdwpub) (at 26 October 2020); and *Ancestry: Jonathan Harris Family Tree – Johanna O'Brien* (http://tinyurl.com/yy397jej) (at 26 October 2020).

397 See *Ancestry: Deaths in the District of Benalla, 1934 – Edward Harris* (http://tinyurl.com/y4oyua7s) (at 26 October 2020); and *The Age*, Saturday, 17 March 1934.

398 See the *North Eastern Ensign*, Friday, 16 March 1934, p. 3.

399 See *Ancestry – Death Certificate for Johanna Harris* (http://tinyurl.com/y4v8st7t) (at 26 October 2020).

400 See *Ancestry: Jonathan Harris Family Tree – Johanna O'Brien* (http://tinyurl.com/yy397jej) (at 26 October 2020).

Walter Harris

Walter Harris was Jonathan Harris' tenth child and his second by Mary Ann Harris. Born in Hobart, he arrived as a baby in Benalla together with his parents and older brother, Edward Harris.[401]

Walter may have worked for a time as an adolescent on his father's Benalla market garden. However, farming of any sort was not to be his vocation. Instead, he took up blacksmithing. It is not presently known whether he was apprenticed to a local Benalla blacksmith or whether he simply went to work for one and thereby learned his trade informally. In any event, it would seem that he worked in Benalla for a number of years as a blacksmith – either as an employee or perhaps on his own behalf.[402]

It would seem that in his youth, Walter was a great sportsman; taking a particular interest in cricket.[403] His membership of Benalla cricket teams probably took him over time to localities surrounding Benalla which he may never otherwise have visited. No doubt it also made him many friends in and around Benalla.

On 17 January 1879, Walter Harris married Catherine Murphy in Nagambie, on the Goulburn River to the south-west of Benalla. Walter was 23 years of age at the time of the marriage.[404] Catherine was 21 years old.[405] Not a great deal appears to be currently known about Catherine's background. It would seem that she was born in 1858 at Winchelsea in south-western Victoria.[406] Presumably, she moved with her parents and siblings to either the Benalla or Nagambie district prior to her marriage to Walter. Where and how they met is not presently known. Walter and Catherine went on to have a total of 10 children. The first, William (Willie) Harris, was born in 1880. The last, Lucy Harris, was born in 1895.[407]

In about 1891, Walter and Catherine moved from Benalla with their children to Baddaginnie. Baddaginnie was then, and remains, a small settlement some 12 km to the east of Benalla. Walter opened up a blacksmithing business in the hamlet.[408]

Life in Baddaginnie was not all work for Walter Harris. A camping trip to Lima, to the south of Benalla, in January 1895 led to legal trouble for Walter and a friend, Thomas Hayes. A cooking fire the two had lit on 13 January 1895 apparently escaped and burned some 50 acres (around 20 hectares) of grassland on the nearby Lima cattle run. On Tuesday, 5 February 1895, Walter and Hayes were each fined £2 in the Benalla Court of Petty

---

401   See footnotes 228 and 230, together with their accompanying texts, above.
402   See Walter Harris' obituary in the *North Eastern Ensign*, Friday, 4 December 1925, p. 3.
403   Ibid.
404   See *Ancestry: Jonathan Harris Family Tree – Walter Harris* (http://tinyurl.com/y2tp32qh) (at 28 October 2020).
405   See *Ancestry: Jonathan Harris Family Tree – Catherine Murphy* (http://tinyurl.com/y4hftd7j) (at 28 October 2020).
406   Ibid.
407   Ibid.
408   See Walter Harris' obituary in the *North Eastern Ensign*, Friday, 4 December 1925, p. 3.

Sessions for leaving the fire unextinguished. The Police Magistrate, C. L. Dobbin, observed in Court that he believed that the two defendants thought that they had put their fire out, but that the Act did not allow for any mistake being made.[409]

It appears that Walter left Baddaginnie in about 1911. He moved with his family to North Wangaratta, where he again established a blacksmithing business.[410] However, ill-health hastened his retirement some seven years later in 1918. It seems that he was afflicted with diabetes. He apparently spent his last years quietly.[411]

During the First World War, two of William's sons, William (Willie) Harris and Albert Ernest Harris, saw service in Europe in the First AIF. Albert Harris was wounded at Passchendaele and later died in England.[412]

Walter Harris died in the Wangaratta Hospital on Saturday, 28 November 1925 of the combined effects of his diabetes and pleurisy. He was 70 years old when he died. He was buried in the Wangaratta Cemetery on Sunday, 29 November 1925.[413] In an obituary published in the *North Eastern Ensign*, Walter was remembered thus:

> "Old residents of Benalla and district will regret to hear the death of Mr Walter Harris, of North Wangaratta, the sad event taking place at the Wangaratta Hospital on Saturday last. The cause of death was pleurisy, following diabetes, from which he had suffered for many years. The late Mr Harris, who had reached the ripe age of 70 years, was a native of Tasmania. When only five years old his family settled in Victoria. Deceased came to Benalla where he resided for a short period after which he opened up business as a blacksmith at Baddaginnie, which he conducted for 20 years. Fourteen years ago he went to North Wangaratta and there he followed his trade. About seven years ago however deceased retired from active life and spent his declining years in retirement in Wangaratta. The late Mr Harris was an expert in all branches of the trade. He was a great athlete in his day and took a keen interest in cricket, being regarded as one of the best bowlers in the district. By his good-hearted disposition he made many friends, all of whom will read of his demise with regret. He is survived by his wife, three sons — Mesrrs William (Thoona), Walter (Melbourne), and Gordon (Wangaratta), and three daughters — Mesdames T.

---

409 See the *North Eastern Ensign*, Friday, 8 February 1895, p. 2.
410 See Walter Harris' obituary in the *North Eastern Ensign*, Friday, 4 December 1925, p. 3.
411 *Ibid.*
412 Albert Harris enlisted in Wangaratta as a private in the 37th Australian Infantry Battalion on 14 January 1916. After being shipped to England, he was assigned to the 37th Australian Infantry Battalion: see Australian War Memorial, *37th Australian Infantry Battalion* (http://tinyurl.com/y49uw2gb) (at 28 October 2020). Sent to the Western Front in Belgium, he was severely wounded in both legs on 12 October 1917 on the opening day of the First Battle of Passchendaele (otherwise known as the Third Battle of Ypres): see *Wikipedia – Battle of Passchendaele* (http://tinyurl.com/y49q6qej) (at 28 October 2020). His left tibia was fractured and gangrene ensued. Albert was taken from the battlefield on 13 October 1917 to 11 Field Ambulance. He was transferred on 14 October 1917 to 2 Canadian Casualty Clearing Station, where part of his left leg was amputated and his other wounds were treated. Albert was then taken to 3 Canadian General Hospital in Etaples, France, where the remains of his left leg were amputated at the thigh. He was finally transferred to the Red House Hospital at Cromer in Norfolk, England on 21 October 1917. There, he was found to be suffering from uraemia in consequence of kidney failure. Albert died on 12 November 1917 and was buried in the Cromer Military Cemetery on 15 November 1917: see National Archives of Australia, *Service Record for Albert Harris* (Series No. B2455) at pp. 6, 13, 14, 16, 24 and 25 (http://tinyurl.com/yxdxbu4e) (at 28 October 2020). According to Albert's *Burial Report*:

"The deceased soldier was accorded a full Military Funeral. The Gun Carriage, drawn by 6 horses, was supplied by the Royal Engineers stationed at Cromer.

The funeral left the Red House Hospital at 2 p.m. and Australian soldier patients followed the remains in 3 mourning coaches.

A Firing Party and Pipe Band was furnished by Cameron Highlanders. A service was conducted in the Cemetery Chapel, and at the graveside by Rev. Davey, The Vicarage, Cromer, Norfolk. The "Lament" was played by a Piper of the Cameron Highlanders. No. 2829 Pte C. V. Harris, 4th Pnr Bn (brother of deceased), Brigadier-General E. Scott-Kerry, Lt. Col. Campbell, Lieut. Wishart, Captain W. K. Anderson, 5th Black Watch, Surgeons Gordon of Sherringham and Grant of Cromer, all the nurses of the Hospital, and members of the Kings Own Scottish Borderers, Black Watch, Seaforth and Gordon Highlanders and Royal Scots were present at the funeral."

See National Archives of Australia, *Service Record for Albert Harris* (Series No. 2455), p. 31 (http://tinyurl.com/yxdxbu4e) (at 28 October 2020). See also *Virtual War Memorial – Albert Harris* (http://tinyurl.com/y6avksav) (at 28 October 2020); and Cathy Sedgwick, *No. 2 Burial Ground, Cromer, Norfolk War Grave – A Harris* (http://tinyurl.com/y4n2nusq) (at 28 October 2020)

413 See Walter Harris' obituary in the *Benalla Standard*, Friday, 4 December 1925, p. 4.

Brown (Numurkah), A. Flegg (Wangaratta) and Bertha (Wangaratta) for whom much sympathy is felt in their loss. Mr E. Harris (Benalla) is a brother of the deceased. The remains were interred in the Wangaratta cemetery on Sunday last."[414]

Catherine Harris died in Wangaratta at the age of 82 years shortly prior to 31 July 1940. She was buried with her late husband Walter in the Wangaratta Cemetery on 31 July 1940.[415]

---

414   See Walter Harris' obituary in the *North Eastern Ensign*, Friday, 4 December 1925, p. 3.
415   See *Ancestry: Jonathan Harris Family Tree – Catherine Murphy* (http://tinyurl.com/y4hftd7j) (at 28 October 2020)

Francis Harris

The first of the children born to Jonathan and Mary Ann Harris in Benalla, and Jonathan's eleventh child overall, was Francis Harris. Francis likely led an ephemeral existence. As mentioned above, he was born on 20 October 1857 and died 38 days thereafter on 27 November 1857.[416]

---

[416] See footnotes 243 and 244, together with their accompanying texts, above.

Albert Harris

Jonathan Harris' twelfth child, Albert Harris, was also his fourth with Mary Ann Harris. Like Francis Harris, Albert was to have a short life which ended tragically.

In common with his older siblings, Albert Harris probably received little, if any, formal education. Like his brothers, Edward and Walter Harris, Albert probably worked from an early age on his father's market garden in Benalla. However, on his *Death Certificate*, he was described as being a labourer.[417] This probably meant that when old enough, he likely obtained a job as a general hand on one of the rural properties surrounding Benalla. The property concerned could well have been in the vicinity of Warrenbayne to the south of Benalla.

In any event, it was near to Warrenbayne that Albert sustained fatal injuries on Wednesday, 17 January 1877 after being thrown from his horse. The circumstances attending his fall were described in the *Evening News* in the following terms:

> "On Wednesday afternoon a most deplorable accident befell a young man named Albert Harris, aged about 19, son of Mr. Jonathan Harris, an old and respected resident of Benalla. The lad was out with two other young men, one of whom was James Belton, of the Warrenbayne sawmill, after cattle when a kangaroo was startled, of which young Harris was soon in pursuit, and in attempting to ride the marsupial down, his horse fell. The poor young fellow was pitched over, alighting on the top of his head either against a stump or the hard ground, where his mates found him in an insensible condition. He was taken to Belton's sawmill, and brought home to his father's residence on Thursday morning. Doctors Henry and Nicholson were both in attendance, but from the terrible nature of the fracture of the skull, very little hopes were entertained, and early on Friday morning the poor lad succumbed to the injuries received."[418]

As indicated in the *Evening News*, Albert Harris died on Friday, 19 January 1877. The official cause of his death was said to be "compression of the brain". He was about 19 years old when he died. Albert was buried in the Benalla Cemetery on Saturday, 20 January 1877.[419]

---

417 See *Ancestry – Death Certificate for Albert Harris, 1877* (http://tinyurl.com/y5rokq7r) (at 29 October 2020).
418 See the *Evening News* (Sydney), Monday, 22 January 1877, p. 2.
419 See *Ancestry – Death Certificate for Albert Harris, 1877* (http://tinyurl.com/y5rokq7r) (at 29 October 2020); and *Ancestry: Jonathan Harris Family Tree – Albert Harris* (http://tinyurl.com/y6rf3mcj) (at 29 October 2020). See also footnotes 245 and 253, together with their accompanying texts, above.

Frances Alice McEwan (née Harris)

Frances Alice Harris was Jonathan Harris' thirteenth child. Like her older brothers, Francis and Albert Harris, Frances was born in Benalla to Jonathan's third wife, Mary Ann Harris.

Although she could apparently read and write, Frances probably received little in the way of formal schooling. It would seem likely that from an early age, she assisted her mother with family and domestic duties in their Benalla home.

On 27 September 1877, Frances Harris married John McEwan in the Holy Trinity Anglican Church in Wangaratta. Frances was only 17 years old at the time of her marriage and secured her father's consent to its occurrence. Her new husband was 26 years old. The official witnesses to the marriage were the bride's parents, Jonathan and Mary Ann Harris.[420]

Frances' husband, John McEwan, was born in 1851 in Adelaide, South Australia to William McEwan and his wife, Mary McEwan (née Hegarty). Following John's birth, his family did not remain for long in South Australia. John's younger siblings were born in Bungaree near Ballarat and in Ballarat East. It seems likely that William McEwan had turned his hand to gold prospecting. However, William had little time to make his fortune on the Victorian goldfields. He died in 1862 on the Caledonia Reef at Golden Square near Sandhurst (now Bendigo) when John was only 11 years of age.[421]

It appears that John McEwan made his career in the Victorian Railways Department. This no doubt took him to various parts of Victoria. Where and how he first met Frances Harris is not now known. In all probability, it was while he was assigned to work for the Railways in Benalla.[422]

It is likely that over time, John McEwan's railway duties saw him assigned to a range of locations in Victoria. After he married Frances, she would have accompanied him with their growing family. In all, Frances and John were to have a total of 12 children. Eight of those children were born in Benalla, three in Colac and one in Tallarook.[423]

By 1904, the McEwan family had moved to Bendigo, where John had been appointed to the position of roadmaster for the railway line between Bendigo and Swan Hill.[424] As roadmaster, John was responsible for the track, bridges, signal and other infrastructure over that length of railway line.

---

420 See *Ancestry – Marriage Certificate for John McEwan and Frances Alice Harris, 1877* (http://tinyurl.com/yylp4xun) (at 30 October 2020).

421 See *Ancestry: Russell Maxwell Family Tree – John McEwan* (http://tinyurl.com/yxms97mg) (at 30 October 2020). See also *Ancestry: Jonathan Harris Family Tree – John McEwan* (http://tinyurl.com/yysvcqmg) (at 30 October 2020).

422 See *Ancestry: Russell Maxwell Family Tree – John McEwan* (http://tinyurl.com/yxms97mg) 9at 30 October 2020).

423 Ibid. See also *Ancestry: Jonathan Harris Family Tree – Frances Alice Harris* (http://tinyurl.com/y3fvgkf4) (at 30 October 2020).

424 See *Ancestry: Russell Maxwell Family Tree – John McEwan* (http://tinyurl.com/yxms97mg) (at 30 October 2020).

However, on 15 June 1904, John McEwan died suddenly. On 16 June 1904, the *Bendigo Independent* announced his death in the following manner:

"The death of Mr. John McEwan, which took place at his residence, Gladstone street, suddenly last night will come as a painful surprise to his many friends. The deceased gentleman, who was roadmaster between Bendigo and Swan Hill on the railways, was 52 years of age, and had been suffering during the last few days from influenza. He was attended by Dr. Deravin and as he was improving, nothing serious was apprehended. Hence his sudden death from heart failure came as an awful shock to his family. He was a native of Adelaide, but had spent 50 years of his life in this State. He leaves a wife and family of six daughters and four sons. The funeral will take place on Friday at 3.30 o'clock, in the Bendigo cemetery."[425]

The edition of the same newspaper published on 18 June 1904 described John McEwan's funeral thus:

"The remains of the late Mr. John McEwan were committed to their last resting place yesterday in the Methodist section of the Bendigo cemetery. There was a large assemblage of friends present who followed the cortege from his residence, "Cleopatra", Gladstone street, Quarry Hill. About 100 railway employees and officials also marched in front of the hearse to the cemetery, where the coffin was borne to the grave By Messrs F. Hillman, J. Leech, C. Pearse, C. Ross, H. O'Brien,, and R. Francis. Service was held at the residence by the Rev. Mr. Judkins, and was conducted at the graveside by the Rev. T. Grove, assisted by the Rev. Mr. Judkins. Among the many beautiful floral tributes was a handsome domed artificial wreath from the railway employees. The funeral arrangements were carried out by Mr. W. Palmer, McCrae street."[426]

Following her husband's death, Frances McEwan lived on for a time in Bendigo before moving to Melbourne. She apparently lived in a number of different Melbourne suburbs with members of her family. she died on Tuesday, 20 August 1940 in the home of a grand-daughter at 37 Phillip Street, Coburg. She was 80 years old when she died. Frances was buried the following day, Wednesday, 21 August 1940 in the Fawkner cemetery.[427]

---

[425] See the *Bendigo Independent*, Thursday, 16 June 1904, p. 3.
[426] See the *Bendigo Independent*, Saturday, 18 June 1904, p. 4.
[427] See *Ancestry: Jonathan Harris Family Tree – Frances Alice Harris* (http://tinyurl.com/y3fvgkf4) (at 31 October 2020); and *The Age*, Wednesday, 21 August 1940, p. 1.

Frederick Harris

Frederick Harris was Jonathan Harris' fourteenth child. Like the last seven of Jonathan's children with his third wife, Mary Ann Harris, Frederick was born in Benalla.

Not a great deal appears to be known about Frederick's life. What is known is that he never married and that he worked as a labourer.[428] What sort of labouring work he performed and who he worked for remain to be discovered. However, it appears that he lived most of his life in the town of his birth: Benalla. According to Margaret Cooper:

> "The house he lived in, up until shortly before his death in 1942, was a small weatherboard house in the style of a miner's cottage, in Garden Street. This may have been Jonathan's original home in Benalla."[429]

Frederick appears to have been close to his younger sister, Charlotte O'Brien (née Harris). An undated photo of Frederick shows him seated beside a timber house in a rural setting, with Charlotte standing by his side. In the photo, Frederick presents as a corpulent man with thick white hair and a prominent moustache.[430] The photo was likely taken beside Frederick's home in Garden Street, Benalla during a visit made by Charlotte.

Frederick Harris died on Thursday, 12 November 1942 of bronchopneumonia. He was 80 years old when he died. His death occurred in Charlotte O'Brien's home at 75 Union Street, Brunswick. Frederick had either moved from Benalla to live with Charlotte shortly before he died or was visiting her when death overtook him. He was buried in the Fawkner Cemetery on Friday, 13 November 1942.[431]

---

428 See *Ancestry – Death Certificate for Frederick Harris, 1942* (http://tinyurl.com/y5zvytrp) (at 31 October 2020).
429 See Cooper, *Biography of Jonathan Harris* (http://tinyurl.com/y6zb2kad) (at 31 October 2020).
430 See *Ancestry – Photo of Frederick Harris with Charlotte O'Brien* (http://tinyurl.com/yyjnoqfs) (at 31 October 2020).
431 See *Ancestry – Death Certificate for Frederick Harris, 1942* (http://tinyurl.com/y5zvytrp) (at 31 October 2020); and *Ancestry: Jonathan Harris Family Tree – Frederick Harris* (http://tinyurl.com/y2kczue8) (at 31 October 2020).

John Phillip Harris

John Phillip Harris was the fifteenth child of Jonathan Harris and the seventh of Mary Ann Harris' nine children. Details of his life appear to remain sketchy. However, it is clear that his horizons extended beyond his birth-place of Benalla.

At some point in time either shortly before or shortly after 1900, John saw fit to travel to New Zealand. Why he did so, where he lived and what he did for a living whilst he was there are presently unknown. However, according to Margaret Cooper, he lived in New Zealand for about seven years.[432]

It would seem that while John Harris was living in New Zealand, he married an Agnes Proud in 1903.[433] It appears likely that Agnes was either a widow or divorced when she married Jonathan. She was probably born Agnes Speirs on 23 August 1871 at Mount William near Wallan Wallan in Victoria; the daughter of James Speirs, a labourer born in Paisley, Scotland, and the latter's wife, Jane Speirs (née Ratcliffe).[434] Details of her first marriage, together with when and how she came to be in New Zealand when she married John Harris, are matters currently clothed in mystery. For some reason which also remains unknown, Agnes went by the name Agnes Young Harris after that marriage.[435] John and Agnes Harris were to have no children together.[436]

At some now presently unknown time after their marriage, John and Agnes returned to Australia. In 1914, they were recorded as living in Benalla Street, Benalla; with John working as a labourer.[437] It may be that he was employed as such with the Victorian Railways. In any event, it was noted on his *Death Certificate* that he had formerly been a railway employee.[438]

During the period between 1914 and 1933, John and Agnes Harris moved to Melbourne. In 1933, they were living in a house at 26 Ashworth Street, Albert Park. On 14 November 1933, Agnes died in the Austin Hospital, Heidelberg. She was about 63 years of age when she died.[439]

John Harris saw out his days in his home in Albert Park. He died on Saturday, 27 January 1945 in the Alfred Hospital, Prahran of a cerebral thrombosis. John was 80 years old when he died. He was buried in the Fawkner Cemetery on Tuesday, 20 January 1945.[440]

---

432 See Cooper, *Biography of Jonathan Harris* (http://tinyurl.com/y6zb2kad) (at 1 November 2020).
433 See *Ancestry: New Zealand, Marriage Index 1840-1937 – John Phillip Harris* (http://tinyurl.com/y4sl2485) (at 1 November 2020).
434 See Births, Deaths and Marriages, Victoria: *Births in the District of Wallan Wallan, 1871 – Agnes Speirs* (No. 12917/1871); and *Ancestry: Australia, Birth Index 1788-1922 – Agnes Speirs* (http://tinyurl.com/yynye4uv) (at 1 November 2020).
435 See *Ancestry: Cole Family Tree – Agnes Young* (http://tinyurl.com/y4y2qb5n) (at 1 November 2020).
436 See *Ancestry – Death Certificate for John Phillip Harris, 1945* (http://tinyurl.com/y6drhkwl) (at 1 November 2020).
437 See *Ancestry: 1914 Australian Electoral Roll, Division of Indi, Subdivision of Benalla – John Phillip Harris and Agnes Young Harris* (http://tinyurl.com/yyrpg36q) (at 1 November 2020).
438 See *Ancestry – Death Certificate for John Phillip Harris, 1945* (http://tinyurl.com/y6drhkwl) (at 1 November 2020).
439 See *The Age*, Wednesday, 15 November 1933, p. 1; *Ancestry: Australia, Death Index, 1787-1985 – Agnes Young Harris* (http://tinyurl.com/y6drdwkp) (at 1 November 2020); and *Ancestry: Cole Family Tree – Agnes Young* (http://tinyurl.com/y4y2qb5n) (at 1 November 2020).
440 See *Ancestry – Death Certificate for John Phillip Harris, 1945* (http://tinyurl.com/y6drhkwl) (at 1 November 2020); and *Ancestry: Jonathan Harris Fam-*

Charlotte Rebecca O'Brien (née Harris)

Charlotte Rebecca Harris was the sixteenth of Jonathan Harris' children, and the second last of those born to Jonathan's third wife, Mary Ann Harris.

Charlotte Harris was lucky to survive to adulthood. On 10 October 1879, she narrowly escaped drowning in the Broken River at Benalla. Her near-death experience was reported in *The Advocate* in the following terms:

> "A GALLANT rescue from drowning by a mere child is an occurrence of interest which deserves special mention, and we (*North-Eastern Ensign*) trust the following facts will be brought under the notice of the Victorian Humane Society. On Friday, 10th inst., as the children were returning home from the State school across the Broken River, a little girl named Charlotte Harris, instead of going by the bridge, endeavoured to cross a log at the rear of the Mechanics' Institute. The log was submerged, and the child took off her boots and stockings, but had only got to mid-stream when she slipped into deep water. One of her school companions, a little girl named Lizzie Guppy, the brave little twelve-year old daughter of Mr. Walter Guppy, president of the Farmers' Union, was, however, equal to the occasion, and without fear plunged in, without divesting herself of any od her clothing, and swam to the rescue of the drowning child, who had already been down twice when seized by her preserver and carried to shore. This action on the part of little Miss Guppy certainly merits the gold medal at least of the Humane Society, and we trust the president of the shire, or some other gentleman, will take steps to recommend the little girl to the notice of the council of that association."[441]

Charlotte was 13 years old when this incident occurred.

Having survived her brush with death, Charlotte Harris married John O'Brien in St Joseph's Catholic Church, Benalla on 24 December 1884. Charlotte was 22 years of age when she married. Her new husband was 23 years old, and was said in the *Marriage Certificate* to be employed in Benalla as a labourer. The official witnesses to the marriage were Charlotte's older brother, Edward Harris, and a Christina McIvor.[442]

John O'Brien was born in Nunawading on 25 January 1865 and christened in neighbouring Box Hill on 25 March 1865. He was the sixth child of Irish immigrants from County Tipperary, John O'Brien and his wife, Johanna O'Brien (née Finn).[443]

---

ily Tree – *John Phillip Harris* (http://tinyurl.com/y4vot6ax) (at 1 November 2020).

441 See *The Advocate* (Melbourne), Saturday, 18 October 1879, p. 10. On 30 September 1880, Charlotte's rescuer, Elizabeth Guppy, was awarded a bronze, and not a gold, medal by the Victorian Humane Society: see *The Age*, Saturday, 23 July 1881, p. 6.
442 See *Ancestry – Marriage Certificate for Charlotte Rebecca Harris and John O'Brien, 1884* (http://tinyurl.com/y34v9jas) (at 1 November 2020).
443 See *Ancestry: Victorian Births Register Entry – John O'Brien, 1865* (http://tinyurl.com/yxlofcvy) (at 1 November 2020).

John was the second Nunawading O'Brien to marry a Benalla Harris. In 1878, his older sister, Johanna O'Brien, had married Charlotte's older brother, Edward Harris, in Wangaratta.[444] Edward and Johanna Harris may well have served as matchmakers for John and Charlotte O'Brien.

Following their marriage, John and Charlotte made their matrimonial home in Benalla. The nature of John's work as a labourer in Benalla is currently not known. Between 1890 and 1909, the couple had a total of 10 children; all of whom were born in Benalla.[445]

In 1891, Charlotte and John O'Brien appear to have been living in Albert Street, Benalla. In that year, it would seem that Charlotte joined other female members of her Harris family in signing the Victorian *Women's Suffrage Petition*.[446] Charlotte and John were still living in Benalla in 1914, although by then they had apparently shifted to a house in Gomalibee Street. John was still working locally as a labourer.[447]

At some time between the birth of their daughter, Frances O'Brien, in 1909 and Frances' early death in 1927, Charlotte and John moved from Benalla to Melbourne.[448] It appears that they acquired a house at 75 Union Street, Brunswick. John O'Brien died in that house on 6 March 1938 of colon cancer and peritonitis. He was 73 years of age. According to his *Death Certificate*, he had seemingly been a watchman after moving to Melbourne.[449] John was buried in the Fawkner Cemetery on 7 March 1938.[450]

Following her husband's death, Charlotte O'Brien lived on for a further 17 years in their Brunswick home. On 12 November 1942, her older, unmarried brother, Frederick Harris, died there while either visiting or living with Charlotte.[451]

Charlotte O'Brien died on Sunday, 7 October 1945 at her home of bronchopneumonia and myocarditis. She was 79 years old at death.[452] On Tuesday, 9 October 1945, Charlotte was buried in the Fawkner Cemetery with her late husband, John O'Brien.[453]

---

444 See footnotes 291 and 392, together with their accompanying texts, above.

445 See *Ancestry: Jonathan Harris Family Tree – Charlotte Rebecca Harris* (http://tinyurl.com/y2oh29wz) (at 1 November 2020); and *Ancestry: Jonathon Harris Family Tree – John O'Brien* (http://tinyurl.com/y6j6hvl4) (at 1 November 2020).

446 See *Ancestry: Women's Suffrage Petition, 1891 – Benalla* (http://tinyurl.com/y6o2w5v4) (at 1 November 2020). See also footnote 264 and the accompanying text above.

447 See *Ancestry: 1914 Australian Electoral Roll, Division of Indi, Subdivision of Benalla – Charlotte Rebecca O'Brien and John O'Brien* (http://tinyurl.com/y5g7go4x) (at 1 November 2020).

448 See *Ancestry: Jonathan Harris Family Tree – Charlotte Rebecca Harris* (http://tinyurl.com/y2oh29wz) (at 1 November 2020).

449 See *Ancestry – Death Certificate for John O'Brien, 1938* (http://tinyurl.com/yxq3c4k7) (at 1 November 2020); and *Ancestry: Jonathan Harris Family Tree – John O'Brien* (http://tinyurl.com/y6j6hvl4) (at 1 November 2020).

450 See *The Age*, Monday, 7 March 1938, p. 1.

451 See footnote 431 and the accompanying text above.

452 See *Ancestry – Death Certificate for Charlotte Rebecca O'Brien, 1945* (http://tinyurl.com/yxqhlz4z) (at 1 November 2020); and *Ancestry: Jonathan Harris Family Tree – Charlotte Rebecca Harris* (http://tinyurl.com/y2oh29wz) (at 1 November 2020).

453 See *The Argus*, Tuesday, 9 October 1945, p. 2.

Lucy Rosetta McLeod (née Harris)

Lucy Rosetta Harris was the seventeenth and last of Jonathan Harris' children, and the last born by Jonathan's third wife, Mary Ann Harris.

Lucy Harris was raised in the family home in Market Street, Benalla. She almost certainly attended the Benalla State School where she would have learned to read and write. It would appear that her parents did not neglect her religious education. On 15 December 1885, the *North Eastern Ensign* noted that at the annual Christmas tree and tea meeting of the scholars attending the Church of England Sunday School at the Rechabite Hall on 11 December 1885, Lucy was one of a number of girls who entertained the gathering with songs. In Lucy's case, the song was *Dreaming of home and mother*. She was 15 years old at the time of this performance.[454]

Lucy's father, Jonathan Harris, died on 4 October 1891, when she was 19 years of age.[455] She no doubt continued living with her widowed mother until her marriage in 1897.

On Wednesday, 1 December 1897, Lucy Harris married Finlay Gordon McLeod in St. Andrew's Presbyterian Church, Benalla. In lieu of her deceased father, the bride was given away by her older brother, Edward Harris.[456] The *Euroa Advertiser* wrote the following description of the wedding:

> "A very interesting ceremony took place in Benalla on Wednesday, when Miss Lucy Rosetta Harris, youngest daughter of the late Mr. J. Harris, was bound in holy wedlock to Mr. Finlay Gordon McLeod, eldest son of Mr. John McLeod of Gooram. The ceremony was performed by the Rev. A. C. McConnan, and took place in the Presbyterian Church. The bride, who was given away by her brother, was tastefully attired in a cream costume with satin and chiffon trimmings, with the usual wreath and veil, and carried a handsome bouquet. The bridesmaids were Miss Moore, in slate silk lustre, cream lace trimmings, hat to match; Miss McLeod, sister of the bridegroom, white muslin, lace and insertion trimmings, hat to match; Miss H. Harris and Miss A. McEwan, nieces of the bride, cream serge, lace trimmings, hats to match; Miss Maggie Pratt, niece of the bridegroom, white muslin, lace trimmings. Mr J. A. McLeod acted as best man. Each bridesmaid wore a handsome gold brooch, gift of the bridegroom. After the ceremony, the bridal party returned to the residence of the bride's mother, where a splendid spread was provided. After partaking of the good things, a toast list was gone through. The Rev. A. C. McConnan proposed 'the bride and groom'. The bridegroom responded in a few nicely-chosen words, and then preparations

---

454 See the *North Eastern Ensign*, Tuesday, 15 December 1885, p. 2. See also Cooper, *Biography of Mary Ann Squire – Convict* (http://tinyurl.com/y3krcxse) (at 4 November 2020).

455 See footnote 260 and the accompanying text above.

456 See *Ancestry: Jonathan Harris Family Tree – Lucy Rosetta Harris* (http://tinyurl.com/y5yenmkj) (at 4 October 2020); *Ancestry: Jonathan Harris Family Tree – Finlay Gordon McLeod* (http://tinyurl.com/y2m7loxs) (at 4 November 2020); and *Ancestry: Australia, Marriage Index, 1788-1950 – Lucy Rosetta Harris* (http://tinyurl.com/y2nqg9sx) (at 4 November 2020).

were made to escort the newly-wedded pair to the station to catch the evening train to Melbourne, where they intend spending their honeymoon. The bride travelled in a handsome costume of blue bengaline, trimmings of shot silk and ribbon to match, and a white hat. In the evening a number of young folks gathered together, and dancing was kept going until the early hours of the morning. The presents were numerous and costly."[457]

Finlay McLeod was born on or shortly before 24 November 1871 in Kilmore.[458] At the time of his marriage to Lucy Harris, Finlay's parents were living at Gooram, a rural locality some 18 km to the south of Euroa, where Finlay's father, John McLeod, would likely have been either farming or employed as a farm labourer.[459]

Finlay McLeod was a blacksmith by trade. It is possible that he was either apprenticed to, or worked for, Lucy's older brother, Walter Harris, in the latter's blacksmithing business at Baddaginnie.[460] This may have been how Finlay came to meet Lucy. Alternatively, they may have met whilst Finlay was plying his trade in Benalla.

Following their marriage, Lucy and Finlay McLeod lived in Garden Street, Benalla until at least the early 1900s.[461] The first four of their five children were born in that town.[462] However, at some stage between 1903 and 1913, Lucy and Finlay moved from Benalla to the Goulburn River Valley. Their fifth and last child was born in that Valley at Tatura.[463]

By 1917, Lucy and Finlay had moved to Shepparton. On 11 August 1917, their eldest son, John Frederick McLeod, enlisted in the First AIF. In his *Attestation Form*, he stated that his parents were then living in Corio Street, Shepparton.[464] However, by 1927, Lucy and Finlay had moved to a house at 38 Marungi Street in Shepparton.[465]

By 1947, the McLeods had purchased a new house at 24 Marungi Street, Shepparton in Lucy's name. However, they purchased the property subject to an existing lease to a Caroline Turner, who was living in the house with her husband and eight children. Lucy was required to bring protracted proceedings in the Shepparton Police Court over the course of some six months in order to secure the ejectment of the Turner family from the premises. The Police Magistrate, Mr. G. S. Catlow, declared in court that it was one of the most difficult cases he had ever had to decide due to a local hosing shortage which had caused great distress and real hardship to both the McLeods and the Turners.[466]

---

457   See the *Euroa Advertiser*, Friday, 3 December 1897, p. 2. See also the *North Eastern Ensign*, Friday, 10 December 1897, p. 3; and Cooper, *Biography of Mary Ann Squire – Convict* (http://tinyurl.com/y3krcxse) (at 4 November 2020).

458   See *Ancestry: Jonathan Harris Family Tree – Finlay Gordon McLeod* (http://tinyurl.com/y2m7loxs) (at 4 November 2020).

459   See footnote 457 and the accompanying text above.

460   See footnote 408 and the accompanying text above.

461   See *Ancestry: 1903 Electoral Roll for the Benalla Polling Place – Lucy Rosetta McLeod and Finlay Gordon McLeod* (http://tinyurl.com/y6cpqfb7) (at 5 November 2020).

462   See *Ancestry: Jonathan Harris Family Tree – Lucy Rosetta Harris* (http://tinyurl.com/y5arsnml) (at 5 November 2020).

463   Ibid.

464   John McLeod enlisted in Shepparton on 11 August 1917 in 8th Reinforcements, 3rd Pioneer Battalion. After being shipped to Europe, he saw service in France in the 59th Battalion. In July 1918, and whilst in France, John contracted pleurisy with effusion. In August 1918, he was invalided to England. He returned to Australia in January 1919. In April 1919, he was found to be totally and permanently incapacitated for employment. John McLeod died in the Austin Hospital on 26 June 1920: see National Archives of Australia, *Service Record for John Frederick McLeod* (Series No. B2455) (http://tinyurl.com/y68l96uo) (at 5 November 2020).

465   See *Ancestry: 1927 Australian Electoral Roll, Division of Echuca, Subdivision of Shepparton – Lucy Rosetta McLeod and Finlay Gordon McLeod* (http://tinyurl.com/y589bob4) (at 5 November 2020).

466   Although the facts remain opaque here, it may well have been that the McLeods had been renting the property at 38 Marungi Street, and that their lease of it had somehow terminated; thus necessitating their purchase of, and move to, the 24 Marungi Street property: see the *Shepparton Advertiser*, Friday 22 August 1947, p. 4; and the *Shepparton Advertiser*, Friday, 19 September 1947, p. 12.

Finlay McLeod died at the age of 79 years on Sunday, 7 October 1951 in the Mooroopna and District Base Hospital. He was buried in the Shepparton on Monday, 8 October 1951.[467]

Lucy McLeod lived on in her home at 24 Marungi Street, Shepparton until just prior to her death. On Tuesday, 5 October 1961, she died in the Mooroopna and District Base Hospital of peritonitis, diverticulitis and the effects of a bowel resection. She was 89 years old when she died. She was buried with her late husband, Finlay McLeod, in the Shepparton Cemetery on Wednesday, 6 October 1961.[468]

Lucy McLeod died 161 years after the birth of her father, Jonathan Harris.

---

[467] See *Ancestry: Jonathan Harris Family Tree – Finlay Gordon McLeod* (http://tinyurl.com/y2m7loxs) (at 5 November 2020); and the *Shepparton Advertiser*, Tuesday, 16 October 1951, p. 6.

[468] See *Births, Deaths and Marriages, Victoria – Death Certificate for Lucy Rosetta McLeod, 1961* (No. 19855/1961); and *Ancestry: Jonathan Harris Family Tree – Lucy Rosetta Harris* (http://tinyurl.com/y5yenmkj) (at 5 November 2020).

Appendix

Ermington, December 28, 1842.

The Honourable The Colonial Secretary
Sydney

Sir,

I beg leave to state to you for the information of His Excellency the Governor the following narrative of Jonathan Harris the elder, a convict, as I hear a memorial has or is about to be presented in form of a mitigation of his sentence of transportation of fifteen years to a penal settlement, passed on him at the Quarter Sessions held at Parramatta on the 10th of September last.

This man was tried and sentenced to be transported for lie for robbery at Horsham, Sussex in the year 1825. Arrived at this Colony in 1826 and was assigned from the ship, the *Marquis of Hastings*, to Mr Charles Thompson Snr of South Creek. In 1832, his wife followed him with three children and on her arrival in that year by some means he obtained a Ticket of Exemption. In 1835, he was in the employ of William Shelley Esquire of Argyle, now a Magistrate, and occupied a small portion of land of that gentleman adjoining my Estate of Lockyersleigh in Argyle.

Shortly after his residing there, I was plundered of a large quantity of wheat, and having heard that Jonathan Harris had sold wheat to various persons, and well knowing he had none to reap, great suspicion was attached to him at the time that he was the party who stole my wheat.

I had stolen about the same time the iron axle of a dray with the wheels from off the body of a dray that was left in one of my paddocks, distant about a mile from Harris's hut. I went myself to his residence and informed him of the robbery, and whilst talking to him, I observed he repeatedly looked to a place called the Sandy Creek that caused me to suspect it was secreted there. I went to my establishment and returned accompanied by my overseer, a Mr Graham, and two of my servants to the Sandy Creek, and after two hours or more search we found the axle and the wheels buried in the sand. This left no doubt in my mind he was the thief or was accessory to the removal, though this would not have been sufficient even to have taken him for summary jurisdiction. I, however, complained and stated these circumstances to Mr Shelley: when he admitted the strong suspicions against Harris, still retained him and employed him conveying supplies from his residence at the Grampian Hills in Argyle to his station on the Tumut River.

In April 1836, I sent a herd of cattle in charge of a young man, an emigrant, a Mr John Stroud, to a place called Mingay on the Murrumbidgee River. On his route between Yass and that place, he met Jonathan Harris driving a team of bullocks with a dray, when Stroud observed he had three of my working bullocks yoked in his team. He asked Harris

how he had come by them, where he replied they had been lent to his son by one of my men at Lockyersleigh. Stroud told him that could not be true as no one could lend him my bullocks except myself or overseer, and therefore he must have stolen them, and asked him to unyoke them. Stroud took possession of the bullocks and drove them on to Mingay with the herd of cattle.

On this being represented to me, I applied to the Bench at Goulburn to have Harris brought before it for the stealing of my bullocks, but most extraordinarily, and though a prisoner of the Crown and living on Mr Shelley's station on the Tumut, he was not taken into custody until ten months afterwards, and only then on my offering a reward of five pounds which I paid when brought to Goulburn, where he was committeed to take his trial at the Supreme Court, Sydney for cattle stealing and was tried before Mr Justice Burton and acquitted from my inability to prove the felonious intent owing to the non-appearance of the principal evidence, Mr Stroud, who, in September 1836, had been found drowned in the Jugiong Creek near Yass. His Honour Mr Burton, in addressing Harris, said the case had failed, still he had heard quite enough to be satisfied that he was a bad character, and directed that the Clerk of the Court should write a letter to the Principal Superintendent of Convicts to receive Jonathan Harris into Government [charge], and that he was of no account again to be assigned or have any indulgences. Owing, I presume, to His Honour going to England shortly after this man's trial, or omission of the Clerk of the Court, Harris obtained his Ticket of Leave in less than a month after his trial and returned to his old residence and employ at Mr Shelley's at the Grampian Hills where he set up and drove about in his gig.

The circumstances attending the death of Mr Stroud were very suspicious as he was a young man of excellent moral character. He had left Yass on the morning of his death and called at a house of refreshment at Bogolong or near it, no public house at that time being beyond Yass, and asked a woman to give him breakfast, and asked her at the same time if she could change a one pound note as otherwise he could not pay her. She could not do so, and he then said it was of no consequence. He would proceed on though the woman pressed him to take breakfast and pay her some other time. He declined and, crossing the Creek where the water would not have taken him to his knees, he is found drowned. However, by what means remains unknown. The money he had in his pocket, about five pounds, gone. The blankets he had strapped to his saddle also gone. The horse and dray [were] found by the creekside by a shepherd . When looking into the Creek, [the shepherd] saw the flash of a coat floating and, drawing it out, found it to be the body of Mr Stroud, as afterwards identified, and up to this time the matter remains wrapped in mystery.

Jonathan Harris, as before stated, had returned to his old residence near my boundary fence, where he became a greater nuisance than ever, keeping a sly grog shop. My farm servants were frequently drunk, and though every precaution and means were taken to detect him, all failed until a sergeant of the 28th [Regiment] stationed at Towrang Stockade went in disguise as a traveller going up the country and was instantly supplied by Harris with spirits. The sergeant laid an information at Wingello before R. Campbell Esquire, brother-in-law of Mr Shelley. As soon as it was known, Harris immediately disappeared by removing to Mr W Shelley or Mr G Shelley's station at the Tumut River, where he remained and kept out of the way for 12 months, though a Ticket of Leave holder and ought to have mustered, which I find he did not, nor was reported.

In December 1841 last year, to my surprise, I found he had again returned to the Grampian Hills and had actually become the tenant of Mr W Shelley's late residence when he [Shelley] having removed to Goulburn. I took an opportunity of remonstrating with Mr W Shelley upon the impropriety of letting his place to such a tenant, as he well knew the annoyance this man had been to me. He merely replied he would let it to those who would pay him and had security given him for the lease.

In September past, Harris and his son, about 21 years of age, came down to Parramatta accompanied by two bullock drivers and two teams and an old man nearly 70 years of age — a shepherd who had been in Mr Shelley's employ who held an order on Messrs Tingcombe and Watkins for £47, which Harris and son, with the other parties robbed the old man of the notes after he had cashed the order. Harris Snr and Harris Jnr were convicted, the former was sentenced to 15 years to a Penal Settlement and the latter ten years to Van Diemen's Land.

It having come to my knowledge that a petition or memorial was or is to be presented to His Excellency the Governor on behalf of these persons, I consider I should be deficient in my duty knowing all these circumstances if I did not make them known.

I have the honour to be
Sir
Your most obedient and humble
Servant
Edmund Lockyer J. P.

Noted by the Governor, Sir George Gipps, in his own handwriting at the side of page one of Major Lockyer's letter:

This will be taken into consideration if any Petition be received from Jonathan Harris or on his behalf.
G. G.
Take care that it is so.

JONATHAN HARRIS' PROXIMATE FAMILY TREE

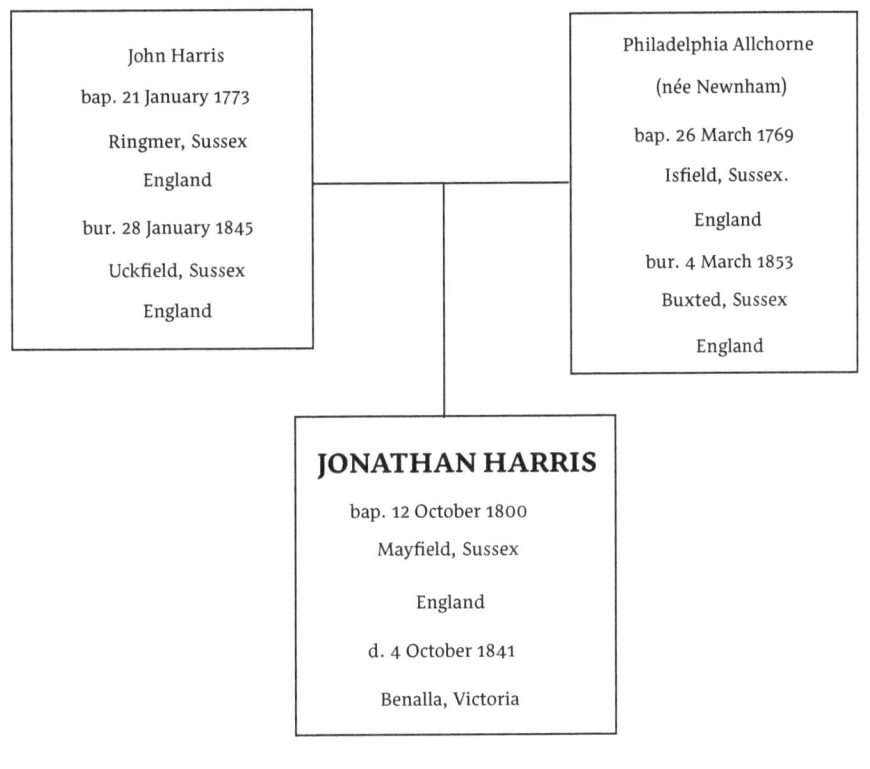

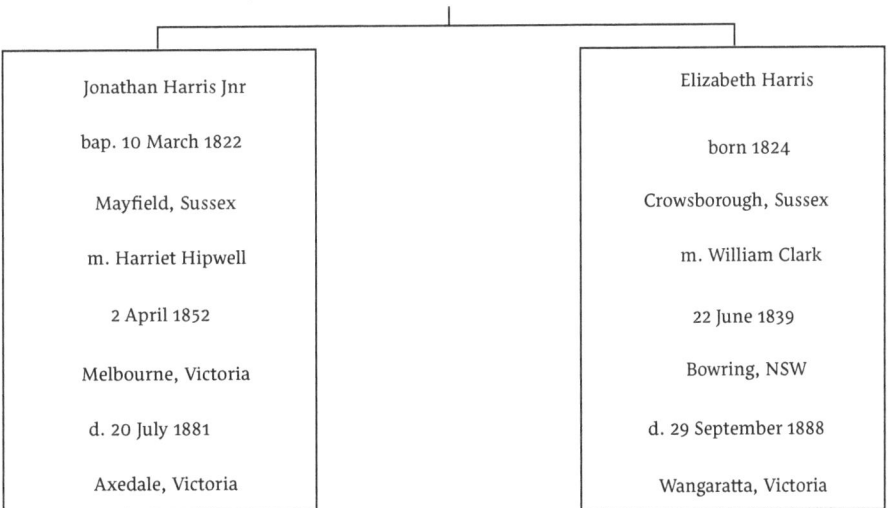

```
                    |
        ┌───────────┴───────────┐
```

Henry Harris

born 1825

Crowsborough, Sussex

d. 9 March 1904

Parramatta, NSW

Sophia Harris

born 15 January 1832

Parramatta, NSW.

1 m. Joseph Young

15 May 1846

Murrays Flat, NSW

2 m. John Povey

c. 1848

Goulburn, NSW

3 m. Alexander Fraser

11 February 1883

North Goulburn, NSW

d. 23 July 1926

Breadalbane NSW

Thomas Harris

born 28 December 1833

Parramatta, NSW

m. Mary Ann Cook

20 February 1837

Melbourne, Victoria

d. 31 July 1924

Carlton, Victoria

George Jarvis Harris

born 19 August 1835

Parramatta, NSW

1 m. Annie Matilda Brown

27 August 1856

Collingwood, Victoria

2 m. Jane Molina Moore

(nee Dawson)

c. 1877

d. 26 June 1928

Kogarah, NSW

JONATHAN HARRIS' PROXIMATE FAMILY TREE

Jonathan Harris married Ann Grubb

22 October 1940

Goulburn, NSW

Jonathan Harris' children with Ann Grubb

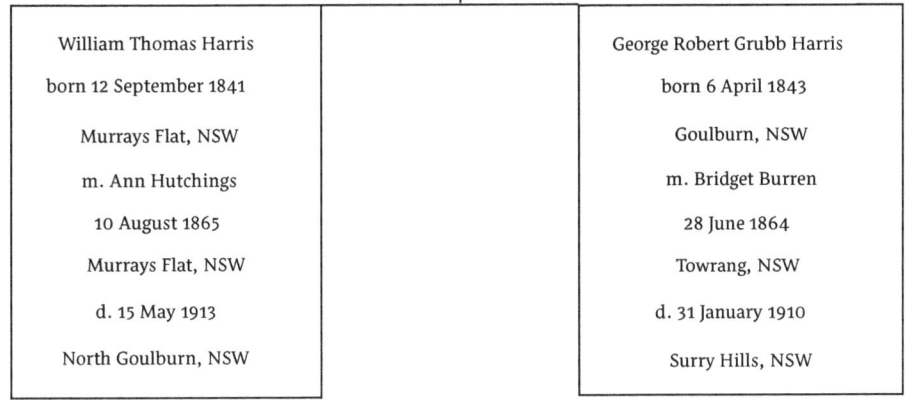

William Thomas Harris	George Robert Grubb Harris
born 12 September 1841	born 6 April 1843
Murrays Flat, NSW	Goulburn, NSW
m. Ann Hutchings	m. Bridget Burren
10 August 1865	28 June 1864
Murrays Flat, NSW	Towrang, NSW
d. 15 May 1913	d. 31 January 1910
North Goulburn, NSW	Surry Hills, NSW

Jonathan Harris married Mary Ann Squire

20 June 1853

Hobart, Van Diemen's Land

Jonathan Harris' children with Mary Ann Squire

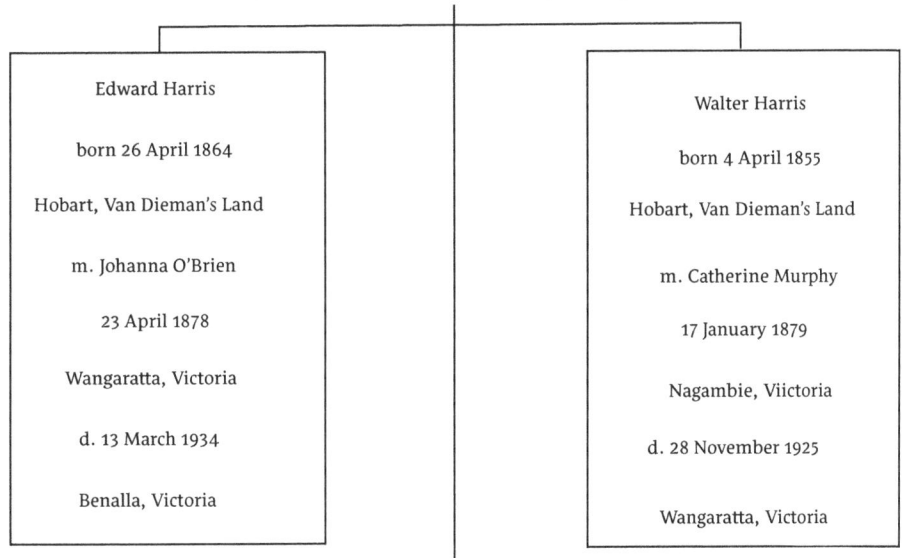

Edward Harris	Walter Harris
born 26 April 1864	born 4 April 1855
Hobart, Van Dieman's Land	Hobart, Van Dieman's Land
m. Johanna O'Brien	m. Catherine Murphy
23 April 1878	17 January 1879
Wangaratta, Victoria	Nagambie, Viictoria
d. 13 March 1934	d. 28 November 1925
Benalla, Victoria	Wangaratta, Victoria

Francis Harris
born 20 October 1857
Benalla, Victoria
d. 27 November 1857
Benalla, Victoria

Albert Harris
born c. 1858
Benalla, Victoria
d. 19 January 1877
Benalla, Victoria

Frances Alice Harris
born 15 July 1860
Benalla, Victoria
m. John McEwan
27 September 1877
Wangaratta, Victoria
d. 20 August 1940
Coburg, Victoria

Frederick Harris
born 23 May 1862
Benalla, Victoria
d. 12 November 1942
Brunswick, Victoria

John Phillip Harris
born 14 June 1864
Benalla, Victoria
m. Agnes Proud
(née Speirs)
c. 1903
New Zealand
d. 27 January 1945
Prahran, Victoria

Charlotte Rebecca Harris
born 30 May 1866
Benalla, Victoria
m. John O'Brien
24 December 1884
Benalla, Victoria
d. 7 October 1945
Brunswick, Victoria

Lucy Rosetta Harris
born 12 March 1872
Benalla, Victoria
m. Finlay Gordon McLeod
1 December 1897
Benalla, Victoria
d. 5 October 1961
Mooroopna, Victoria

East Sussex Map

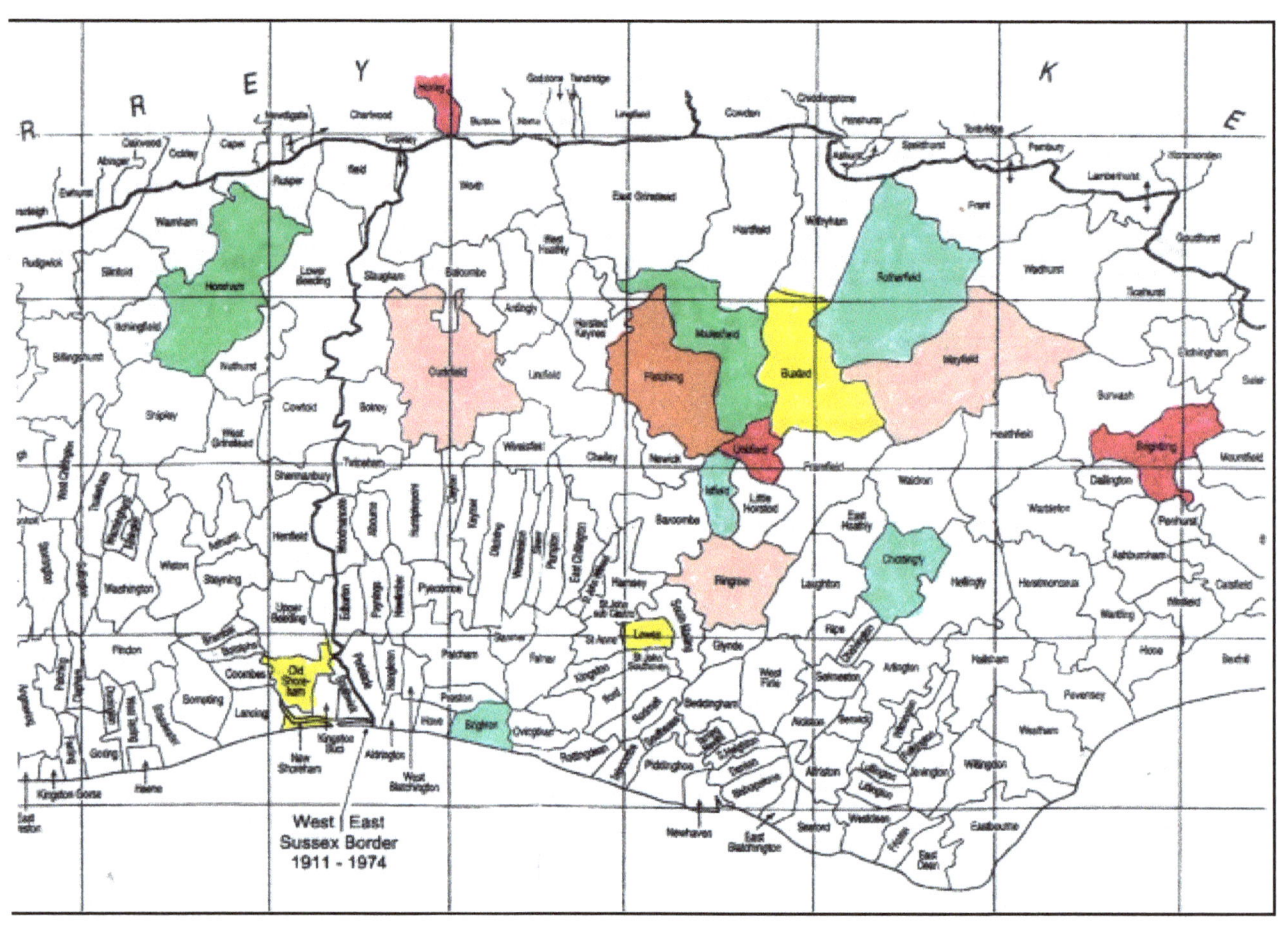

Map of Sussex Parishes Associated with Philadelphia Newnham and her Family Members

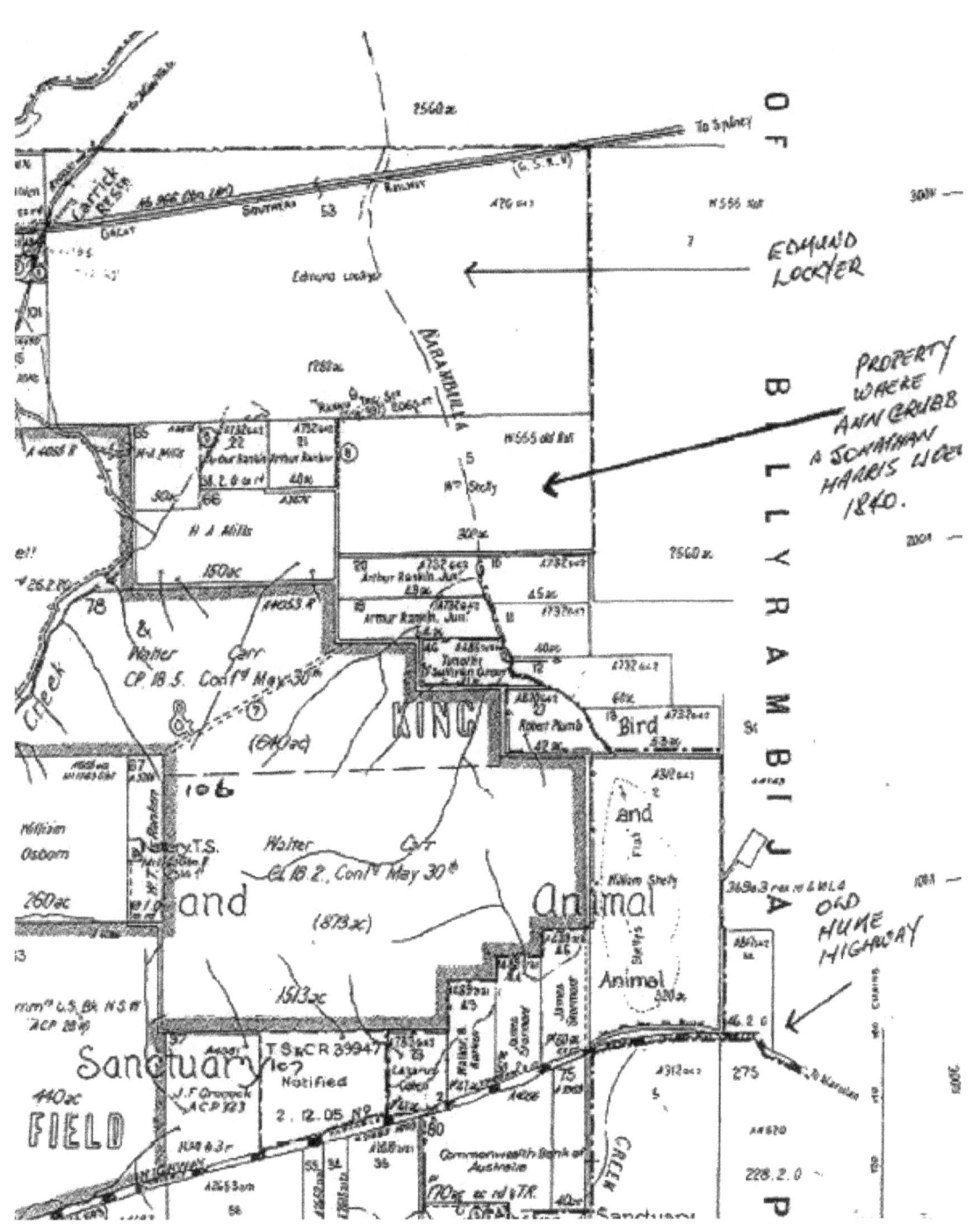

Goulburn Plains Plan

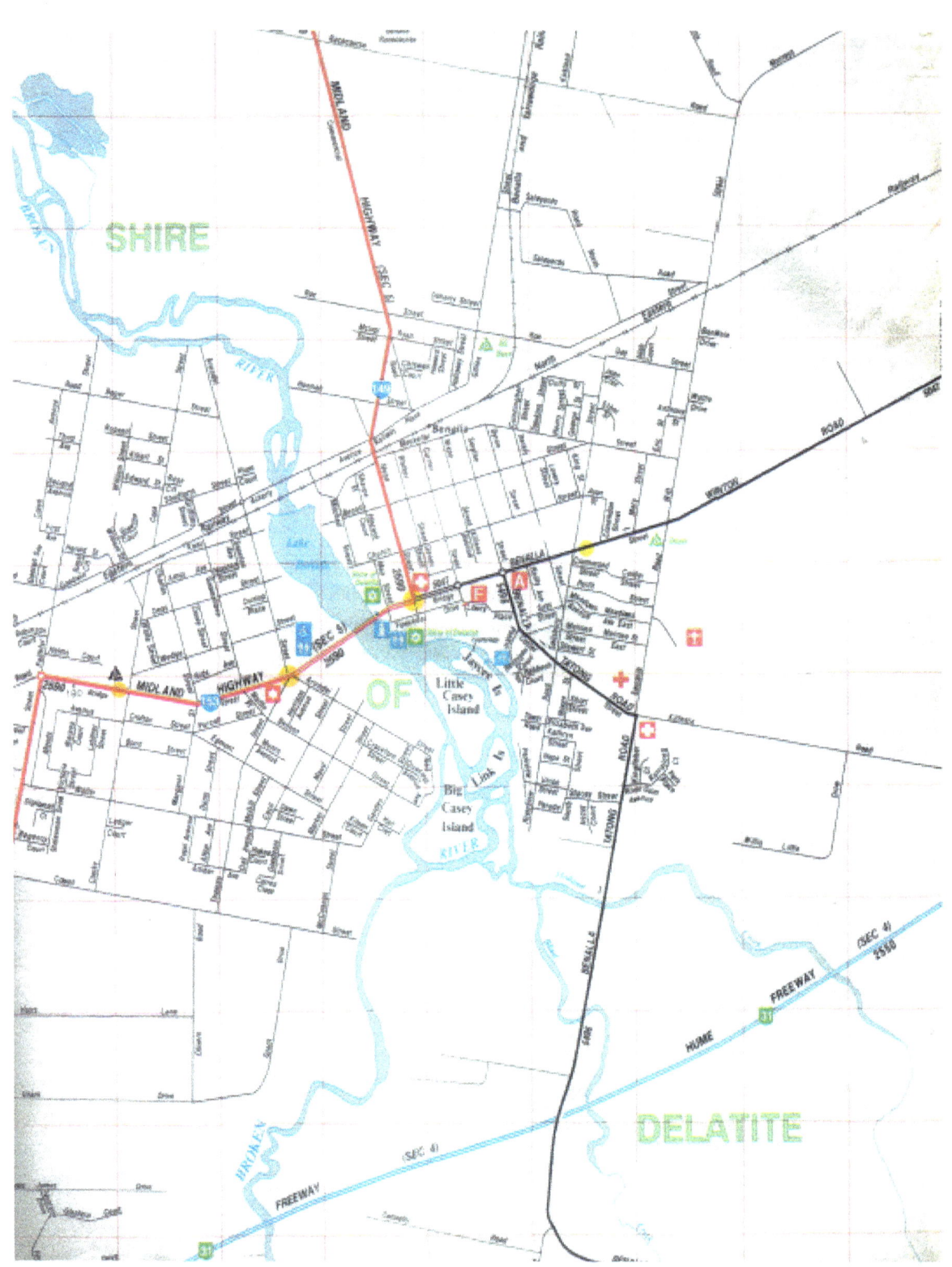

Benalla Map

Photo 1. St Dunstan's Church, Mayfield, Sussex

Photo 2. Entrance to the Lewes House of Correction

Photo 3. Lewes House of Correction (under demolition, 1963)

Photo 4. Sketch of Horsham Gaol

Photo 5. Prison Hulk York

Photo 6. Model of the York Prison Hulk

Photo 7. Model of the York Prison Hulk (cutaway)

Photo 8. Painting of the Hyde Park Barracks (c. 1820)

Photo 9. A Government Gaol Gang, Hyde Park Barracks (c. 1830)

Photo 10. Clydesdale House

Photo 11. Major Edmund Lockyer

Photo 12. Darlinghurst Gaol from the air (c. 1930)

Photo 13. Cockatoo Island Prison

Photo 14. Port Arthur in 1840

Photo 15. The Commandants Cottage, Bridgewater Convict Station

Photo 16. St. George's Anglican Church, Battery Point, Hobart

Photo 17. Jonathan Harris as an old man

Photo 18. Harris graves in the Benalla Cemetery

www.ingramcontent.com/pod-product-compliance
Lightning Source LLC
Chambersburg PA
CBHW061536010526
44107CB00066B/2881